BAPTISM IN THE
NEW TESTAMENT

STUDIES IN BIBLICAL THEOLOGY

A series of monographs designed to provide the best work in biblical
scholarship both in this country and abroad

Advisory Editors:

STUDIES IN BIBLICAL THEOLOGY

BAPTISM IN THE NEW TESTAMENT

OSCAR CULLMANN

Translated by
J. K. S. REID

SCM PRESS LTD
BLOOMSBURY STREET LONDON

The *English version of*
DIE TAUFLEHRE DES NEUEN TESTAMENTS
(Zwingli-Verlag Zürich)

334 00068 8
First published 1950
by SCM Press Ltd
56 Bloomsbury Street London
Second impression 1951
Third impression 1952
Fourth impression 1954
Fifth impression 1956
Sixth impression 1958
Seventh impression 1961
Eighth impression 1964
Ninth impression 1969
Tenth impression 1973

© SCM Press Ltd 1950

Printed in Great Britain by
Fletcher & Son Ltd, Norwich

CONTENTS

FOREWORD

I HAVE intended for a long time to write something about the New Testament doctrine of Baptism. The general discussion of the justification of infant Baptism which has been provoked by Karl Barth's booklet on *The Teaching of the Church concerning Baptism* forbids me to wait any longer. I hold it for an error to deal with the question of infant Baptism in isolation, as has too often happened in Church discussions. I can therefore only deal with this live problem of the day (and not of the day only) according to my original plans, within the framework of a complete review of the matter.

I have already developed the fundamental thought of chapter 1 in 1942 in the *Revue de Théologie et de Philosophie* (Lausanne) under the title ' La Signification du baptême dans le Nouveau Testament ' ; while the appendix on the traces of an ancient baptismal formula in the New Testament has already appeared in the *Revue d'Histoire et de Philosophie religieuses* (Strasbourg), 1937, p. 424ff, and in the first edition of *Urchristentum und Gottesdienst*, 1944.[1]

Chapters 2-4, which are decisive for the question of infant Baptism, are new. I intended originally to incorporate this work in the new and revised edition of my *Urchristentum und Gottesdienst* now appearing (*Abhandlungen zur Theologie des Alten und Neuen Testaments*, No. 3), but chapters 2-4 ran to a greater length than I had foreseen. Moreover an independent reply worked out from the standpoint of New Testament theology seemed to me to be demanded by the importance attached to Barth's treatise, as also by the work of Joachim Jeremias, *Hat die älteste Christenheit die Kindertaufe geübt?*, appearing in 1938 and laying the foundation for Barth's study, and the more recent work of H. Grossmann, *Ein Ja zur Kindertaufe*, 1944.

Barth's study of Baptism arouses attention and alas ! threatens to precipitate schism ; and this is not to be ascribed only to the authority which as a theological teacher he rightly enjoys. His

[1] The second edition does not contain this appendix.

7

study is in fact the most serious challenge to infant Baptism which has ever been offered. Even from the side of the great Anglo-Saxon Baptist Church, from which have sprung so many important theologians, and which in other fields of theology has played so important a part, no equally fundamental defence of the standpoint opposing infant Baptism is known to me.

Yet the more I study the question of New Testament baptismal doctrine, the more the conviction grows in my mind that at this point my respected colleague and friend has developed a view which, though better grounded, is finally not less erroneous than that of all opponents of the biblical character of infant Baptism, ancient or modern. It is not *prior* ecclesiastical or theological interest that brings me to this judgment but purely the New Testament enquiry that is demanded of us. As I explain in the concluding note, I did not myself foresee all these consequences.

CHAPTER ONE

THE FOUNDATION OF BAPTISM IN THE DEATH AND RESURRECTION OF CHRIST

HOW far is Jesus Christ the founder of primitive Christian Baptism? It is not enough here to refer to Matt. 28. 19. This word of the resurrected Christ contains only the demand for Baptism, but does not explain its connection with his person and his work. Judaism already knows of the baptism of proselytes coming over from heathenism. John the Baptist holds all Jews to be like proselytes and demands a baptism to forgiveness of sins from them all, in view of the impending appearance of the Messiah. Baptism as an external act is thus not the creation of Jesus. In this respect it differs from the other sacrament of the Christian Church, the Lord's Supper, whose external form goes right back to Christ. But the connection between Christ and Baptism appears even looser when we consider that Jesus himself did not baptise, at least not during his public work.[1]

Thus the situation is as follows: John the Baptist, following the practice of Jewish proselyte baptism, himself also baptised; Jesus did not baptise; after his death, the primitive Church again baptised. Is this therefore simply a reversion to Johannine baptism? How does Baptism administered by the Apostles differ from that administered by John, which also resulted in forgiveness of sins? What is new in primitive Christian Baptism, and how far is it traceable to Jesus, even if in his lifetime he neither offered it to others nor 'founded' its external form?

John the Baptist himself in the proclamation of his message

---

[1] It is true that the Johannine Gospel (3. 22) emphasises that he did baptise. But in the next chapter (4. 2) this statement is corrected by the affirmation that it was not Jesus, but his disciples, that baptised. This verse is perhaps a marginal gloss. In this case the affirmation of 3. 22 could refer to a period when Jesus himself was still a disciple of John the Baptist. However this may be, Jesus did not administer Baptism during his public appearance.

explained the difference between his own and Christ's Baptism in the following terms : ' I indeed baptise you with water unto repentance : . . . he shall baptise you with the Holy Ghost, and with fire ' (Matt. 3. 11 ; Luke 3. 16). The fire probably alludes to the day of judgment. The Baptism which Christ brings is thus not only preparatory and transitory but final, and will lead directly into the Kingdom of God. But in the meantime, while the disciples are alive in the time between the resurrection and the Parousia of Christ, the important thing in the Baptism administered through the Messiah is the impartation of the Holy Spirit. This is the eschatological gift which is even now realised (ἀπαρχή, ἀρραβών) ; and so Mark limited himself to mention of the Holy Spirit only (Mark 1. 8).

This is then the new element in Christian Baptism according to the preaching of the Baptist. This new baptismal gift of the Holy Spirit is imparted neither by Jewish proselyte baptism nor by Johannine baptism. It is bound up with the person and the work of Christ. In the course of the Gospel story, the outpouring of the Holy Spirit ' on all flesh ' (Acts 2. 17) presupposes the resurrection of Christ and follows on Pentecost. It follows that *Christian* Baptism is only possible after the Church is constituted as the locus of the Holy Spirit. The Book of Acts speaks thus of the first Christian Baptisms in the context of the Pentecostal story. There Peter concludes his sermon, in which he explains the Pentecostal miracle, with the demand : ' Repent, and be baptised every one of you in the name of Jesus Christ ' (Acts 2. 38). What happened in a collective manner at Pentecost is in future to take place for each individual in the sacrament of the transmission of the Spirit.

Why does the transmission of the Spirit within the Church take the form of a Baptism ? Why is it further bound up with the immersion for the forgiveness of sins that John already practised, following the precedent of proselyte baptism ? What has the Holy Spirit to do with purification by water or with immersion in water ? It was understandable that proselyte baptism and Johannine baptism should be represented as an act of washing, because its effect was forgiveness of sins. Just as ordinary water takes away the physical uncleanness of the body, so the water of baptism will take away sins. On the other hand, it is not obvious why the fulfilment of Johannine baptism, as brought about by the Messiah in spiritual Baptism, should still consist in *immersion*, instead of creating for itself a new form.

It is therefore to be asked whether Johannine baptism to the remission of sins is really abrogated by the Christian sacrament of the Spirit. Has the Holy Spirit nothing more to do with the forgiveness of sins ? It is stated in the Pentecostal sermon of Peter already mentioned (Acts 2. 38) : ' Be baptised every one of you in the name of Jesus Christ *for the remission of sins, and ye shall receive the gift of the Holy Ghost.*' Christians still need forgiveness of sins, even in the Church ; it is not enough that the gift of the Holy Spirit be offered to them. Hence the Christian sacrament of the Holy Spirit, prepared and proclaimed in Johannine baptism, remained a Baptism, an immersion, although the sacramental gift of the Holy Spirit has strictly nothing to do with the external act of washing.

The connection in Christian Baptism between forgiveness of sins and transmission of the Spirit is, however, more deeply rooted. It is not simply as if a new element, the imparting of the Holy Spirit, were added to the old immersion for the forgiveness of sins. The new element rather concerns the fulfilment of just this forgiveness of sins, and this in the closest connection with the transmission of the Holy Spirit.

We ascertain from Acts that at a certain moment the primitive Church felt the need of adding to the external act of immersion another particular act specially concerned with the Holy Spirit : the laying on of hands. It appears then that two external acts correspond to the two effects of Baptism, the bath to the forgiveness of sins, and the laying on of hands to the gift of the Holy Spirit. Baptism might thus have run the danger of falling apart into two different sacraments. This did not actually occur, because the firm anchorage which the two baptismal effects had in the fact of Christ averted such a split. This we shall find to be theologically explained in Rom. 6, and to be based on Jesus' own Baptism. But the baptismal stories of Acts prove the danger ever present. For example, the story of the mission to Samaria (ch. 8). Here at verse 12 we read : ' But when they believed Philip preaching the things concerning the kingdom of God, and the name of Jesus Christ, they were baptised, both men and women.' In verses 14ff we learn that the Apostles on hearing this news sent Peter and John from Jerusalem to Samaria. They prayed that those who had been baptised with water might now also receive the Holy Spirit, ' for,' so the story runs, ' as yet he was fallen upon none of them ; only they were baptised in the name of the Lord Jesus. Then laid they their hands on them and they received the Holy Ghost.'

Baptism with water to the forgiveness of sins and laying on of hands for the imparting of the Holy Spirit are here temporally separated and are transmitted by different people. Again, in Acts 10. 44 we find Baptism threatened by the danger of falling apart into two acts. Here we have the inverse order of events : the Spirit is imparted to the heathen (without laying on of hands) ; then they receive Baptism by water. Finally, Acts 19. 1ff should be mentioned. The reference is to the disciples at Ephesus. Paul asks them : ' Have you received the Holy Ghost, since ye believed ? And they said unto him, We have not so much as heard whether there be any Holy Ghost.' Paul then asks them : ' Unto what then were ye baptised ? And they said, Unto John's baptism.' Then they let themselves be baptised in the name of Jesus. Paul lays his hand on them, and the Holy Spirit comes upon them, and they speak with tongues.

The danger could here emerge that one of the two effects of Baptism, namely forgiveness of sins, might be regarded simply as a vestige from the past without real connection with the new gift in Christ, the Holy Spirit. In St. John's Gospel we have perhaps indications that in the primitive Church the danger was recognised and guarded against. For it is emphasised (John 3. 3-5) that one cannot be born again of water only, but of water and the Spirit.[1]

The Jewish Christian texts contained in the Pseudo-Clementines prove besides that at the beginning of the second century there was in fact a Jewish Christian minority for whom Baptism had reverted to the status of a Jewish rite.

The problem of the relation between Baptism by water and the sacrament of the Spirit occupied the ancient Church for a long time.[2] What has the Spirit to do with water? Tertullian found it needful to propose a solution in his treatise on Baptism.[3] He was at pains to demonstrate the essential relation between the Holy Spirit and water, referring to Gen. 1. 1, where it is said that in the beginning the Spirit of God hovered over the waters. This is why the Spirit from then on is bound up with water; and hence Baptism as Baptism of the Spirit has to do with water.

But this is not the correct solution to the problem of the connection of forgiveness of sins, transmission of the Holy Spirit, and Baptism by water. This solution is rather indicated in Jesus' own Baptism by John, as we shall see; and Paul gave it theological expression in Rom. 6. 1ff. This makes it clear that Christian Baptism, when regarded as Baptism for the forgiveness of sins, is no mere reversion to Johannine baptism. It is rather the fulfilment, which became possible only through the completed work of Jesus on the Cross. It is further this work that joins the two effects of Baptism so closely together. As Paul in the sixth chapter of Romans shows, this means that our individual

---

[1] The words ὕδατος καί are attested by all the good MSS. R. Bultmann (*Kritisch-exegetischer Kommentar über das NT. Das Johannesevangelium*, 1938, p. 98, n. 2) suggests their exclusion. This is congruous with his general tendency to regard or explain all allusions in the Fourth Gospel to the sacraments as interpolations. This tendency, however, appears to me to conflict with the cardinal message of the Johannine Gospel. See my treatment in *Urchristentum und Gottesdienst*, 2nd edn., 1948.

[2] Heb. 6. 2 should be remembered here, where the doctrine of Baptisms (βαπτισμῶν in the plural) is named as the foundation of Christian instruction, and laying on of hands is added to it.

[3] De baptismo, ch. 3.

13

participation in the *death and resurrection of Christ* results from Baptism.[1] Here everyone obtains participation in the forgiveness of sins which Christ has achieved once for all upon the Cross. This is no mere development of Johannine baptism. According to Rom. 6. 5 we are in the act of Baptism a single plant with Christ, inasmuch as we die and rise with him.

The external act of βα πτίζειν then becomes significant for both the effects of the Baptism that is based on Christ. Thus too a new relation is formed between the external act of βα πτίζειν and the forgiveness of sins. It is no longer merely the bath, the washing away, that purifies, but the immersion as such : in the act of Baptism the person being baptised is in immersion ' buried with Christ ' (v. 4), and with his emergence follows also his resurrection.[2] Thus the relation between the two effects of Baptism is represented in connection with this act. For being buried with Christ means forgiveness of sins, and the emergence from this burial with him means ' walking in newness of life ' (v. 4) ; and this is not other than the ' walking in the Spirit ' of Gal. 5. 16. Both effects are essentially bound up with one another as is the death of Christ with his resurrection.

Thus the anchorage of Baptism in the work of Christ has three consequences : the forgiveness of sins proclaimed before Christ is now based on the redemptive death of Christ ; forgiveness of sins and transmission of the Spirit come to stand in a close theological connection ; and both are set in a new and significant

---

[1] It is interesting in this connection to mention that Paul in I Cor. 11. 26 reminds the congregation that even the Lord's Supper stands in relation to the death of Christ. We know of course that in certain circles of primitive Christianity the danger of forgetting this was present. The legitimate rejoicing which characterised the primitive Christian celebration of the supper and which was evoked, according to Acts 2. 46, by the living memory of the Easter appearance of Christ, might well at times degenerate (I Cor. 11. 21) and thrust the thought of the death of Christ completely into the background (see *Urchristentum u. Gottesdienst*, 1st edn., p. 13ff).

[2] The affinity with analogous rites of the mystery religions cannot be denied (see especially A. Dietrich : *Eine Mithrasliturgie*, 1903, p. 157ff) ; R. Reitzenstein : *Hellenistische Mysterienreligionen*, 3rd edn., 1927, p. 259 ; F. Cumont : *Les religions orientales dans le paganisme romain*, 1907 ; C. Clemen : *Religionsgeschichtliche Erklärung des Neuen Testaments*, 1924, 2nd edn., p. 168ff). But for the question dealt with here this analogy has no relevance.

relation to one and the same external baptismal act, so that both the immersion and the emergence become significant.

The parallelism between 'being baptised' and 'dying with Christ,' whose origin goes back to the life of Jesus at his own Baptism by John in Jordan, is traceable through the whole of the New Testament and is not limited to Rom. 6. 1ff. We find it first in Paul himself in I Cor. 1. 13, where Baptism is clearly conceived as participation in the Cross of Christ. 'Was Paul crucified for you, or were ye baptised in the name of Paul?' Here the two expressions 'you were baptised' and 'another was crucified for you' are treated as synonymous. This uniformity of expression shows us also that it belongs to the essence of Christian Baptism in the New Testament, that it is Christ that operates, while the person baptised is the passive object of his deed.

The same conception appears in the Epistle to the Hebrews. The impossibility of a second Baptism is in 6. 4f based on the fact that Baptism means participation in the Cross of Christ: 'it is impossible for those who were once enlightened (i.e. baptised), and have tasted of the heavenly gift, and were made partakers of the Holy Ghost . . ., If they shall fall away, to renew them again unto repentance ; seeing they *crucify* to themselves the Son of God afresh.' We see again how here also the transmission of the Spirit is bound up with the redemptive death of Christ for the forgiveness of our sins.

In the Johannine writings indirect traces of the connection of the water of Baptism with the blood of Christ can be at least detected.[1]

The fundamental nature of the relation of Baptism to the

[1] Here chapter 19. 34 and I John 5. 6, and also John 3. 14ff and John 13. 1ff, are especially to be remembered. See *Urchristentum u. Gottesdienst*, 1st edn., pp. 73ff, 49ff, 68ff. I hope I have established the connection between Baptism and the Lord's Supper in chapter 19. 34 (and 13. 1ff) (against R. Bultmann op. cit. ad loc, and recently W. Michaelis : *Die Sakramente im Johannesevangelium*, 1946). But here, as also in I John 5. 6, the relation between the Baptism and the death of Jesus is present, so that we have to do with a kind of triangular relation, which indeed does not appear to me to be foreign to Johannine thought.

death of Christ for New Testament baptismal doctrine is, however, wholly evident only when we put this question concerning the meaning of Baptism, which Jesus himself raised with John the Baptist at Jordan. What does his own Baptism mean to the historical Jesus? This is a question which came before the ancient Church. Why did Jesus, despite his sinlessness, submit himself for Baptism? The baptism of John was meant for sinners. The Gospel of the Ebionites and that of the Hebrews concern themselves with this question. The Gospel according to St. Matthew also puts John's question at the climax of the story (3. 14): ' I have need to be baptised of thee, and comest thou to me ? ' And Jesus answers : ' Suffer it to be so now : for thus it becometh us to fulfil all righteousness.'

In the synoptic account of Mark and Matthew (Mark 1. 10f and Matt. 3. 16f) and, according to well-attested versions, also Luke (3. 22), the answer is contained in the event itself, namely in the proclamation of the heavenly voice : ' Thou art my beloved Son, in whom I am well pleased.' It is of the greatest importance for the understanding of the Baptism of Jesus, and hence of the so-called ' messianic consciousness of Jesus,' that his heavenly voice consists in a citation from Isa. 42. 1. That is, we here have a reference to the Ebed-Jahwe songs. The servant of God, who must suffer vicariously for his people, is in this manner addressed in the Old Testament.

The manuscript D, with some other witnesses from the so-called Western Text, offers a variant here for the Lukan text. According to this manuscript, the voice sounded otherwise : ' Thou art my beloved Son, today have I begotten thee.' This would be a citation not from Isa. 42. 1 but from Ps. 2. 7, the familiar 'Royal Psalm.' This passage is in fact quoted in Acts 13. 33 (and also Heb. 1. 5 and 5. 5), where it is related to the resurrection, not to the Baptism. In this Psalm the King is addressed as God's Son. Christians have here seen scriptural proof for the divine Sonship of Christ, since in virtue of his resurrection he has entered into Kingship. In Acts 13. 33 the reference is in fact to the resurrection of Christ, and here this citation from the Royal Psalm is in its right place. From here it may have found its way into Luke's account of the Baptism in the manuscripts mentioned, though it is at least possible that in Luke it is original. Even if this is the case, the Mark-Matthew version is to be preferred here. According to it, Christ at his Baptism is not yet proclaimed King but only the servant of God. His Lordship appears later, after his resurrection ; but first of all he has to complete the work of the suffering Servant of God in direct connection with the meaning of Johannine baptism, and in fulfilment of this meaning.

The form of words of the heavenly voice in the Greek diverges from Isa. 42. 1 only in one respect. παῖς would be the correct rendering of the Hebrew *abdi*, ' my servant,' and this correct translation appears in the quotation of the same passage in Matt. 12. 17. But instead of παῖς, it is υἱός that stands here. The affinity of the Greek words παῖς and υἱός and the connection of the Hebrew words *bachir* and *jachid* with the Greek roots ἀγαπητός, ἐκλεκτός and μονογενής suggest that Jesus was first addressed as υἱός in the Greek translation of Isa. 42. 1, while in the Semitic original he is designated as *ebed*, servant, which corresponds with the text of Isa. 42. 1. This possibility must certainly be reckoned with, especially at John 1. 34, a passage which, as we shall see, has a connection with the heavenly voice, and offers as a well-attested variant not the word υἱός but ἐκλεκτός, which is the usual translation in the Septuagint for the Hebrew *bachir*, by which the *ebed* of God is designated in Isa. 42. 1. But even if the Hebrew form of the heavenly voice already contained the word ' Son,' in contrast to Isa. 42. 1, still the rest of the context refers to Isa. 42. 1, the well-known beginning of the Ebed-Jahwe song,[1] and Jesus is then designated Son, in so far as, in the rôle of Servant of God, he takes the guilt of his people

---

[1] F. Leenhardt : *Le baptême chrétien*, 1944, p. 27, n. 2, thinks that the word ἀγαπητός originates neither from Isa. 42. 1 nor from Ps. 2. 7. But Matt. 12. 17, where Isa. 42. 1-4 is also cited, has ὁ ἀγαπητός μου.

upon himself in his suffering and death. For he who is addressed in Isa. 42. 1 has certainly to fulfil the mission which is more closely described in the 53rd chapter of Isaiah.

For an understanding of the deeper meaning of the Baptism of Jesus it is significant that Jesus at the very moment when he is baptised hears this voice, which offers him the title of Son, according to the Greek text—and in any case (and this is the decisive consideration) the title of that Son who will fulfil the mission which in the Old Testament is prophetically ascribed to the suffering Servant of God.

Here we find the answer to the question : What meaning has Baptism to the forgiveness of sins for Jesus himself in the New Testament ? At the moment of his Baptism he receives the commission to undertake the rôle of the suffering Servant of God, who takes on himself the sins of his people. Other Jews come to Jordan to be baptised by John for their *own* sins. Jesus, on the contrary, at the very moment when he is baptised like other people hears a voice which fundamentally declares : *Thou art baptised not for thine own sins but for those of the whole people.* For thou art he of whom Isaiah prophesied, that he must suffer representatively for the sins of the people. This means that Jesus is baptised in view of his death, which effects forgiveness of sins for all men. For this reason Jesus must unite himself in solidarity with his whole people, and go down himself to Jordan, that ' all righteousness might be fulfilled.'

In this way, Jesus' answer to the Baptist, ' to fulfil all righteousness' (πληρῶσαι πᾶσαν δικαιοσύνην, Matt. 3. 15), acquires a precise meaning. The Baptism of Jesus is related to δικαιοσύνη, not only his own but also that of the whole people. The word πᾶσαν is probably to be underlined here. Jesus' reply, which exegetes have always found difficult to explain, acquires a concrete meaning : Jesus will effect a general forgiveness. Luke (like Mark) does not use this word, but he emphasises in his own way the same fact at 3. 21 : ' Now when *all* the people were baptised' (ἄπαντα τὸν λαόν), Jesus also was baptised.' It is clear in view of the voice from heaven why Jesus must conduct himself like other people. He is distinguished from the mass of other baptised people, who are baptised for their own sins, as the One called to the office of the Servant of God who suffers *for all others*. The suffering Servant of God is, like the Messiah, already known to Judaism. But that the Messiah should be *at the same time* the suffering Servant of God is an impossible conception for Judaism. It is true that the Messiah occasionally bears the title of Servant of God; but the representative suffering that is characteristic of the Ebed Jahwe is never ascribed to him. The Targum at Isa. 53 is most instructive at this point.[1] Connection between the two is first made through the life of Jesus.

Thus the Baptism of Jesus points forward to the end, to the climax of his life, the Cross, in which alone all Baptism will find its fulfilment. There Jesus will achieve a general Baptism. In his own Baptism in Jordan he received commission to do this.

This explanation is confirmed by the meaning which the word βαπτίζειν has for Jesus. We have seen that Jesus did not himself baptise. Now we understand better the reason for this abstinence. For him, to ' be baptised ' from now on meant to suffer, to die for his people. This is not a pure guess; it is confirmed by each of the two sayings in which Jesus uses the word βαπτίζεσθαι: Mark 10. 38 and Luke 12. 50. In Mark 10. 38, 'can ye be baptised with the baptism that I am baptised with?', ' be baptised ' means ' die.' See also Luke 12. 50: ' I have a baptism to be baptised with; and how am I straitened till it be accomplished ! ' Here also ' be baptised ' means just ' die.' On both occasions it is Jesus who speaks. In the reference of the word ' baptise ' to death it is his own death that is implied. Only in a derivative way can the same expression be extended also to the disciples. It is he, Jesus, who will not only baptise individual men with water like John the Baptist but will complete the *general* Baptism, for all men, and once for all, at the moment of

[1] See on this P. Seidelin: *Der Ebed Jahwe und die Messiasgestalt im Jesajatargum* (Z.N.T.W., 1936, p. 197ff).

his atoning death. *It belongs to the essence of this general Baptism effected by Jesus, that it is offered in entire independence of the decision of faith and understanding of those who benefit from it.* Baptismal grace has its foundation here, and it is in the strictest sense ' prevenient grace.'

After the death and resurrection of Jesus the disciples again administer individual Baptism with water. The meaning of this is to be investigated more closely in the next chapter. But in any case it is already clear why this individual Baptism is not a reversion to Johannine baptism but can only be a Baptism into the death of Christ. Now we understand better how it is that Christian Baptism in the New Testament is participation in the death and resurrection of Christ. Now we know the deepest roots of the baptismal doctrine of Rom. 6. 1ff, which can also be traced throughout the whole New Testament.

Confirmation that Christian Baptism is thus founded upon the life of Jesus, and may be traced back to the Baptism of Jesus in Jordan, is to be found in the Gospel according to St. John 1. 29-34. This passage is, so to speak, the first commentary upon the synoptic account, and it appears that the author of the Fourth Gospel has understood it in the sense of our exposition. Reference in St. John's Gospel to the Baptism of Jesus is made in the form of μαρτυρία, of evidence which John the Baptiser of Jesus depones *after* the event. This is not recounted as a fact but is presupposed and turned to account. The evidence is comprised in the word in verse 29: 'Behold the lamb of God which taketh away the sin of the world.' In verse 33 the Baptist remembers that he has seen the Holy Spirit descend and rest upon Jesus, and he adds in verse 34 the conclusion: 'I saw, and bare record that this is *the elect of God*.' Here is a clear reference to the voice from heaven which sounded at Jesus' Baptism in order to designate Christ with the expressions of Isa. 42. 1. The reading ἐκλεκτός, of which we have already spoken,[1] is best attested by the Sinaiticus, the *vetus itala* and the

----
[1] V. sup. p. 17.

Old Syriac translation; in the other manuscripts ἐκλεκτός is replaced by υἱός, in order to harmonise the text with the synoptics. We have seen that ἐκλεκτός is the usual translation which the Septuagint gives of the Hebrew word *bachir* which appears in Isa. 42. 1.

While the relation of the Baptism of Jesus to his representative suffering and death is apparent in the synoptic account only in the context of the voice from heaven which refers to Isa. 42. 1, the Johannine Gospel is clearer at this point. The Baptist draws a conclusion from the heavenly voice and declares that Jesus is ὁ ἀμνὸς τοῦ θεοῦ ὁ αἴρων τὴν ἁμαρτίαν τοῦ κόσμου. Thus he rightly understood the call as a demand upon Jesus to fulfil the Ebed-Jahwe mission.[1]

If we thus interpret the Gospel account of the Baptism of Jesus from the standpoint of the heavenly voice, according to its meaning for salvation history, an indirect light is cast on the New Testament connection between the two effects of Christian Baptism, forgiveness of sins and imparting of the Spirit. The Synoptics like the Johannine Gospel show how Christian Baptism, so far as it is Spirit Baptism, has its basis in Jesus' Baptism in Jordan. At his own Baptism Jesus himself also received the *Spirit*, in all its fulness. This also stands in relation with the atoning suffering of the Servant of God in Isaiah. In the Old Testament, that is, in Isa. 42. 1, the second half of the text, whose beginning is contained in the voice from heaven, runs thus : ' I have put my spirit upon him [the Servant of God] : he shall bring forth judgment to the Gentiles.' We thus find that in the Old Testament possession of the Spirit is prophesied

---

[1] The connection between ὁ ἀμνὸς τοῦ θεοῦ and *ebed Jahwe* is even plainer if we not only reflect that in Isa. 53. 7 the servant of God is compared to a lamb but also pay attention to the philological fact which is emphasised by C. F. Burney : *The Aramaic Origin of the Fourth Gospel*, 1922, that the Aramaic equivalent for ἀμνὸς τοῦ θεοῦ, *thaljah delaha*, means both ' lamb of God ' and ' servant of God.' Also the Aramaic equivalent for αἴρω, *nathal*, can also mean φέρειν, which would form an even closer connection between the ἀμνὸς τοῦ θεοῦ of John 1. 29 and the voice from heaven which referred to the *ebed-Jahwe*. But even apart from these considerations this relation stands sufficiently firm.

in the same verse as the suffering Servant of God. On the basis of this Spirit, Christ will complete the δυνάμεις, and hence Matthew rightly sets the miracle of Christ in relation to Isa. 42. 1-4 and Isa. 53. 4.[1]

In respect also of the two effects of Christian Baptism, Jesus' Baptism in Jordan directs us to the climax of his work : to his death and his resurrection. The temporal connection of Christian Baptism with the death and resurrection of Christ is thereby also affirmed. Christian Baptism becomes possible only from the moment when these salvation events are completed. John 7. 39 is to be remembered here : ' the Holy Ghost was not yet given ; because that Jesus was not yet glorified ' ; and also John 16. 7 : ' if I go not away, the Comforter will not come unto you.'

Individual participation in the death and resurrection of Christ in Baptism is possible only after Christ has completed his general Baptism ; and this is the reason why he himself was baptised by John, and why those received into the Church today are baptised.

We have seen that Christian Baptism is in fact practised only after Pentecost.

That this is the hour of the birth of Church Baptism is congruous with the temporal course of salvation history : the atoning work of Christ is completed here. The temporal centre of all history, the death and resurrection of Christ, is also the centre of the history of Baptism. But Pentecost represents the decisive turning point for the subsequent course of this history, not only because it completes the salvation events but also because the further unfolding of salvation history begins from here. The Church is constituted here as the locus of the Holy Spirit, as the Body of Christ crucified and risen. Thus the baptismal death of Christ completed once for all on the cross passes over into Church Baptism.

The next chapter will show how they are related.

[1] See Matt. 8. 16-17 and 12. 17-22.

CHAPTER TWO

BAPTISM AS ACCEPTANCE INTO THE BODY OF CHRIST

WE have seen that, according to the New Testament, all men have in principle received Baptism long ago, namely on Golgotha, at Good Friday and Easter. There the essential act of Baptism was carried out, entirely without our co-operation, and even without our faith. There the whole world was baptised on the ground of the absolutely sovereign act of God, who in Christ 'first loved us' (I John 4. 19) before we loved him, even before we believed. What does it mean then, when Baptism is performed by the Church? Is it not a superfluous activity if Christ has already died and risen for everyone at that historical moment in time which for believers represents the centre of the ages?

Most theologians today agree that the distinctive element in the baptismal act of the primitive Church at first consisted in the relation of that act to the individual who now dies and rises again with Christ (Rom. 6. 3). On the other hand, the explanations diverge widely as soon as the attempt is made to define more closely the nature of that relation and thus to establish what it is in the Baptism of an individual that effects his participation in Christ's death and resurrection. According to Karl Barth, who here adduces a statement of Calvin, Baptism in the New Testament is a matter of the *cognitio* of salvation, so that it is quite impossible to speak of 'effecting' in the proper sense. The individual is merely 'made aware.' Along with the definition of the baptismal act as a *cognitio*, the question of infant Baptism is also implicitly raised, and as a matter of course answered in the negative. For it is meaningless to impart knowledge concerning Christ's death and resurrection to an infant, and the answer of faith, which is the only possible response to this knowledge, is for him out of the question. Karl Barth is therefore right when he constructs his denial of the Biblical character of infant Baptism upon this interpretation. Whoever regards it as correct will have difficulty in defending infant Baptism.

This interpretation, however, does not appear to me to do justice to the New Testament facts, and I shall oppose it with another based on the New Testament texts. All discussions about Baptism should begin with this question, viz. with the theological definition of the essence and meaning of Baptism. It is in fact necessary to ask whether infant Baptism is attested by our primitive Church sources. Now the New Testament texts allow us to answer *this* question with certainty in neither one way nor the other, and we must simply accept this fact. Even the passages which speak of the Baptism of ' whole houses ' allow no unambiguous conclusion to be drawn, at least in this respect. For we do not in fact know whether there were infants in these houses. These passages may be used only to explain the *doctrine* of Baptism. They are not effective proof of the practice of infant Baptism in apostolic times. The defenders of the Biblical character of this practice ought not to make their task easy by claiming forthwith its proof by the mention of ' whole houses.'

But on the other hand, neither should those who dispute the existence of primitive Christian infant Baptism rely on the view that nowhere in the New Testament is infant Baptism mentioned. For it is certain that in a missionary Church like the New Testament Church, i.e. at the time of its emergence, the opportunity for such a practice would seldom occur even if it were in thorough agreement with primitive Church doctrine. Such opportunities would occur only in two quite different cases : first, when a whole house in which there were infants came over into the Christian Church ; and secondly if, after the conversion and Baptism of the parents or of one of the parents, children were born, a case not ordinarily occurring at the very earliest beginnings, but certainly in New Testament times.

Baptism as Acceptance into the Body of Christ

It is the weakness of almost all opposition to infant Baptism that it does not distinguish these two quite different cases. The very way in which they were distinguished in proselyte baptism in contemporary Judaism ought to prevent us ignoring this question. The penetrating historical references which Joachim Jeremias provides in this regard, in a work which is of the greatest importance for the whole question,[1] cannot be overlooked in this discussion. When heathen came over into Judaism, their children also were subjected along with them to proselyte baptism. On the other hand, such children as were born only after the conversion of their parents did not have to be baptised. They ranked as sanctified through their parents, an important consideration in view of the analogy in I Cor. 7. 14.[2]

At least the *possibility* of an *indirect* proof of primitive Christian infant Baptism seems to be demonstrated by the careful explanations of Jeremias. Consideration should also be given here to the form in which the account in Mark 10. 13ff. (Matt. 19. 13ff. ;

---

[1] J. Jeremias : *Hat die älteste Christenheit die Kindertaufe geübt?*, 1938. Mention should also be made here of A. Oepke : *Zur Frage nach dem Ursprung der Kindertaufe* (Festschrift für Ihmels), 1928, and Johannes Leipoldt : *Die urchristliche Taufe im Lichte der Religionsgeschichte*, 1928, works which are fundamental for the study of the relation between primitive Christian Baptism and proselyte baptism. Based on these works, especially the first named, are Giovanni Miegge : *Il Battesimo dei Fanciulli nella storia, nella theoria, nella prassi*, a penetrating investigation accorded too little attention by us, which arose out of the discussions of the Waldensian Church in 1942 ; and Hermann Grossmann : *Ein Ja zur Kindertaufe* (Kirchliche Zeitfragen, vol. 13), 1944, who takes account of works representing an opposite standpoint by K. Barth and F. J. Leenhardt : *Le baptême chrétien, son origine, sa signification* (Cahiers théologiques de l'Actualité protestante, No. 4), 1944. A similar standpoint to H. Grossmann's is occupied by Albert Schädelin : *Die Taufe im Leben der Kirche* (Grundriss, 1943, p. 177ff). Recently there has appeared the essay by Théo Preiss : *Le baptême des enfants et le Nouveau Testament* (Verbum Caro, 1947, p. 113ff), which comes to the conclusion that infant Baptism is in harmony with the New Testament doctrine of Baptism. See also M. Goguel : *L'Eglise primitive*, 1947, p. 324ff). Unhappily the important contributions, which have just appeared in Holland and which take up a position against Barth's booklet, cannot be referred to again here : G. C. Berkouwer : *Karl Barth en de kinderdoop*, 1947 ; G. C. van Niftrik : *De kinderdoop en Karl Barth* (Nederlands Theologisch Tijdschrift, 1947, p. 18ff).

[2] See (Strack-) Billerbeck : *Kommentar zum Neuen Testament aus Talmud und Midrasch*, Vol. I, 1922, p. 110ff.

Luke 18. 15ff.) of the blessing of the children is transmitted.[1] More need not be added to this. While I deliberately express myself with all possible caution concerning the historical question of the practice of infant Baptism in the New Testament, I should like, on the other hand, with all force to emphasise at the outset that there are in the New Testament decidedly *fewer traces, indeed none at all, of the Baptism of adults born of parents already Christian and brought up by them.* Chronologically such a case would have been possible about the year 50, if not earlier, that is, certainly within New Testament times. The only case of the children of Christian parents of which we hear occurs in I Cor. 7. 14, and agrees with the practice of proselyte baptism, where only children of heathen actually converted to Christianity are baptised, not those born only after the conversion of their parents. In any case, this passage excludes a later baptism of these Christian children at adult age.

Those who dispute the Biblical character of infant Baptism have therefore to reckon with the fact that *adult Baptism for sons and daughters born of Christian parents, which they recommend, is even worse attested by the New Testament than infant Baptism* (for which certain possible traces are discoverable) *and indeed lacks any kind of proof.*

But the question must be put from another standpoint than that of evidence. The position is that it can be decided only on the ground of New Testament *doctrine* : Is infant Baptism compatible with the New Testament conception of the essence and meaning of Baptism ? The great value of the brochure by Karl

[1] See Appendix, p. 71ff. on the Traces of an ancient Baptismal Formula in the N.T. (an essay of mine first published in *Revue d'Histoire et de Philosophie religieuses*, 1937, p. 424). There I point out the influence exercised by the liturgical baptismal ' terminus technicus ' κωλύειν on the form of this account. Independently and by another road Jeremias (op. cit., p. 25) comes to an analogous conclusion ; but he starts not as I do from Mark 10. 14 but from Mark 10. 15, and shows that Mark like John 3. 3 and 5 connects the summons to repentance of Matt. 18. 3 with Baptism, and uses the words ὡς παιδίον in the sense of ' as a child.' Jeremias has collated both explanations in a reference in the *Z.N.W.* (1940) under the title ' Mark 10. 13-16 and parallels and the Practice of Infant Baptism in the Primitive Church.'

Barth lies in this, that it deals with the question in this way. It has at least the merit of calling the Church to reflect on the meaning of Baptism. But even if, as it seems to me, the answer given reveals very important and hitherto neglected aspects, it is not true to the New Testament in its essential conclusions.

The question should be formulated from the declared standpoint of New Testament theology strictly as a problem of New Testament exegesis. It must certainly not be confused with the question of ' National or Confessional Church ' (*Volkskirche oder Bekenntniskirche*). With his ' hinc, hinc illae lacrimae,'[1] Karl Barth objects that the defenders of infant Baptism are motivated solely by the effort to preserve the National Church by means of infant Baptism. This may perhaps be applicable to many advocates of infant Baptism. But in reading Barth's expositions, the question occurs whether the ' hinc, hinc illae lacrimae ' could not find an inverted and opposite application to Barth himself in his legitimate concern to realise a Confessional Church. Is not the opposition to infant Baptism, a practice which he characterises as a ' wound in the body of the Church,' [2] employed by him to some extent in the service of *this* cause ?

When the question ' National or Confessional Church ' is confused with the definition of Baptism, the whole problem is from the start thrust into a perspective which does not belong to the New Testament. It cannot be disputed that *consequences* for what is called the ecclesiological problem follow from the examination of the essence and meaning of Baptism. All I need say in this matter is that, if one is concerned to ascertain the decisive features of the practice of infant Baptism, he cannot handle the texts dealing with infant Baptism when the question is given a form so foreign to the New Testament.

Of course, the Church into which the person baptised is received has a confessional character in the New Testament. It is also true that the Baptisms of adults who come over from Judaism

[1] Op cit., p. 53.　[2] Op cit., p. 40.

and heathenism, i.e. the only Baptisms of which we certainly hear in the primitive Church, as a rule give occasion for affirmation of faith on the part of the adults being baptised. But it is a mistake to conclude too hastily either that the confessional character of the primitive Church is tied to Baptism, or that faith and confession are preconditions of a significant and regular Baptism. Concerning the first, one must say that *adult* Baptism in primitive Christianity is indeed an important occasion for confessing the faith ; but it is certainly not the only occasion, and the confessional character of the Church does not stand or fall with it. The faith was probably always confessed at divine service in the primitive Church ; and profession of it is also made before the judges, at exorcisms of spirits, in the teaching of the Church,[1] and perhaps also in commissioning someone to duties in a congregation. Concerning the second, the connection between faith and Baptism, as we shall see in the next chapter, faith is indissolubly connected with the act of Baptism. But this connection must be defined exactly. In no case should the fact be ignored that in adult Baptism this faith must be present at the moment of the baptismal act, and that the constituent element of the connection between faith and Baptism is precisely this temporal or rather contemporary accompanying faith.

The necessity of separating the question of infant Baptism from the question of ' Confessional or National Church ' arises also from the consideration that, long before Constantine, Irenæus affirms infant Baptism, and yet he certainly stands within a ' Confessional Church.'[2]

F. Leenhardt maintains in his work on Baptism[3] that infant Baptism is fundamentally a quite different sacrament from adult Baptism. He refers to the fact that it is customary to cite, as Biblical foundation for infant Baptism, New Testament texts which do not speak of Baptism at all, while the New Testament

---

[1] See my *Die ersten christlichen Glaubensbekenntnisse* (Theol. Studien, Vol. 15), 1943 (in English *The Earliest Christian Confessions*, Lutterworth, 1949).
[2] As H. Grossmann, op. cit., p. 27, rightly says.
[3] Op cit., p. 69.

texts which do speak of Baptism do not apply to infant Baptism. This judgment of F. Leenhardt is to be explained by his conception of the meaning of Baptism which is akin to Karl Barth's conception, and which fails to do justice to its proper meaning. We shall on the contrary ascertain that the proper doctrine of Baptism in the New Testament is quite compatible with infant Baptism, whether it was practised or not, and that conversely those other New Testament texts which are adduced to establish infant Baptism can also find a legitimate application to adult Baptism.[1] Hence the importance of being quite clear what really is the theological meaning of the *individual's* dying and rising with Christ in the act of baptism, after the decisive general Baptism for *all* men is achieved at Golgotha.

Here it seems to me right to begin with the difference between Baptism and Holy Communion. It is possible to show[2] that in the primitive community the Church engaged in only two types of Church service : Holy Communion and Baptism, the first certainly including proclamation of the Word. In the Eucharist the community also participates in the death and resurrection of Christ. What then distinguished Baptism and the Eucharist from one another ? In another place I have shown[3] that it is of the essence of the Eucharist that it is *repeated*, whereas Baptism *cannot be repeated* for the individual. But for the question of the meaning of Baptism we must add that in the Eucharist it is the constituted *community*, in Baptism the *individual* inside this community, to whom the death and resurrection are related.

Thus Barth's objection that admission to the Eucharist would have to be administered to infants[4] after their admission to Baptism becomes invalid. The meaning of this *repeated* appropriation of the death and resurrection of Christ by the community in the Eucharist is defined by its relation to the unique act of

[1] A. Schädelin, op. cit., p. 182, emphasises that Baptism when extended to infants does not become a different sacrament.
[2] O. Cullmann : *Urchristentum und Gottesdienst*, 1st edn., p. 24ff.
[3] Op. cit., pp. 72 and 77.
[4] K. Barth, op. cit., p. 52.

Baptism. The meaning is that here there gather, to the exclusion of the unbelieving and the not-yet-believing, *those who already believe* and who again and again assure themselves of their salvation as a community in the act of the Eucharist. In Baptism, on the other hand, the individual is, for the first time and once for all, set at the point in history where salvation operates—where even now, in the interval between his resurrection and the Second Coming, the death and resurrection of Christ, the forgiveness of sins and the Holy Ghost, are according to God's will to be efficacious for him. This *once-for-all character of being set at this specific* place, i.e. within the Church of Christ, is what distinguished Baptism from Communion, while the participation in the death and resurrection of Christ is what connects them.

In Rom. 6. 3ff Paul describes *what* takes place in Baptism : the person baptised is ' planted ' with the dead and risen Christ. In I Cor. 12. 13 he defines more clearly *how* precisely this participation in the death and resurrection of Christ in Baptism proceeds : ' by one Spirit are we all baptised into one body.' From the previous verse it is evident that this body is the Body of Christ, and from the whole context that this Body of Christ is the community, i.e. the Church. To determine the essence and the meaning of Baptism, *both* these passages, Rom. 6. 3ff and I Cor. 12. 13, must be taken together. The latter contains an unambiguous answer to the question from which we set out : what *specific thing* does the act of Baptism in the primitive Church mean, if we are all already baptised at Golgotha ?

The connection of the two texts Rom. 6. 3ff and I Cor. 12. 13 is not arbitrary. An inner bond exists between them, in so far as the Body of Christ into which we are baptised is at the same time the crucified body of Christ (Col. 1. 24; II Cor. 1. 5; I Pet. 4.. 13) and his resurrected body (I Cor. 15. 20-22). On the basis of a like connection of thought between death and resurrection with Christ on the one hand, and the building up of a community of Christ on the other hand, Paul in Gal. 3. 27-28 (a most important baptismal text) says also : ' as many of you as have been baptised into Christ *have put on Christ* . . . ye are all one in Christ.'

On the other hand, among the passages in the New Testament where Baptism is mentioned didactically, there is not one where information about the saving acts of Christ or *cognitio* (as Barth says and as F. Leenhardt fundamentally agrees[1]) is regarded as the specific event of the once-for-all act of Baptism. I find no passage where it is said or hinted that we have to seek in *cognitio* the special content of the act of Baptism that goes beyond the historical event of Golgotha. Admittedly the New Testament accounts for the most part refer to the person baptised as an adult, who comes to faith before Baptism, and naturally declares this faith by confession.[2] But nowhere do we hear that this *cognitio* constitutes what really happens in Baptism. On the contrary, what happens in the act of Baptism is clearly defined in the decisive Pauline texts I Cor. 12. 13 and Gal. 3. 27-28 as a setting within the Body of Christ. God sets a man within, *not merely informs him that he sets him within*, the Body of Christ ; and *at this moment* therefore the reception of this act on the part of the person baptised consists in nothing else than that he is the passive object of God's dealing, that he *is really set within* the Body of Christ by God. He ' is baptised ' (Acts 2. 41), an unambiguous passive.[3] Whatever the other considerations to which Baptism gives rise, they are to be subordinated to this definition and to be explained by it. Barth also speaks quite emphatically of the building up of the Church in Baptism. But the decisive fact is that he attributes no effective power to this act of God *as such*. Instead he finds the grace of Baptism in the *declaration* of this act and its reception by faith. Of course, the Church must proclaim what God accomplishes in Baptism. But this does not mean that

[1] Op cit., p. 69.

[2] V. App., p. 71ff. For the fact that the oldest liturgy mentions this confession of faith, v. inf., p. 52.

[3] So far in opposition to F. Leenhardt. Op. cit., p. 57, however, also says : le baptême est le sacrament par lequel l'Eglise *se recrute*.

God's characteristic operation in Baptism in and for the Church has a ' cognitive significance.'

The Eucharist is also something that happens to the Body of Christ. But we have seen above that it is characteristically distinguishable from the event of Baptism. In the very same chapter of the first Epistle to the Corinthians (10. 16ff), it is said that the fellowship of the breaking of bread is a fellowship within the Body of Christ, and that we, the many who partake of one bread, are *one* Body. In the Eucharist the Body of Christ is not increased by the addition of new members who are ' added ' (Acts 2. 41), but as the Body of Christ the existing congregation is always newly strengthened in the deepest meaning of the term. But in the act of Baptism something different happens to the Body of Christ : it is quantitatively increased through the ' addition ' (προσετέθησαν) of those who ' are baptised into the body of Christ.' This increment is an event of the greatest importance for the Body of Christ also, and it thus concerns not only the individual, as is usually said, but also the Church as a whole. With every Baptism a new victory is won over the hostile powers, as a new member is set at the place where he can be delivered from these powers.

In this sense, I can emphasise what Barth says about the ' glorifying of God in the upbuilding of the Church of Jesus Christ.'[1] But why should not this glorification, as such and apart from ' cognitive significance,' have causal efficacy for the individual ?

As on Golgotha, so here it is God who operates in Christ. Indeed this ' addition ' is an absolutely *free* work of God, independent of both our human state and our faith. Church Baptism would acquire a fundamentally different character from that of the general Baptism accomplished by Jesus at Golgotha, if God's operation were dependent on the human acts of faith and confession, while in fact the deepest significance of the atonement is precisely that it is accomplished without any kind of co-operation,

[1] Op cit., p. 32.

and even against the will, against the knowledge, against the faith of those for whom it is effective.[1] If in the Baptism of the Church faith is primarily not a *subsequent answer* to God's work but a precondition of God's dealing with us, Golgotha and Church Baptism as acts of reception into the covenant of grace lie no longer on the same level. We shall have to speak in the next chapter of the rôle which faith plays in Baptism, and of the significance of the fact that the presence of faith in the person being baptised before and during his Baptism is so often mentioned. Here we are concerned to show that Baptism at Golgotha and Baptism into the Church are connected *in their innermost essence* as divine acts wholly independent of men. It is of the essence of both that faith must *follow* as answer to the divine act. In the case of *Church Baptism*, faith must also *follow*, even if faith in the general Baptism at Golgotha is already present before the act completed in water, as is the rule in the case of the Baptism of adults in the New Testament. Church Baptism in this case also demands a faith which can only follow the act of Baptism, faith, that is to say, in the specific thing which now happens in the presence of the Church : *the ' addition ' of a new member to the Body of Christ crucified and risen.* If faith of this kind does not follow upon Baptism, then the divine gift comprised within it is disdained and dishonoured, and its fruits destroyed. The gift itself, however, retains its reality, being dependent not on the individual's acknowledgement of faith in Christ but on Christ's confessing this individual through his incorporation into his Church, and his receiving him into the special fellowship of his death and resurrection.

Everything that the New Testament implicitly teaches concerning a *gratia praeveniens* (Rom. 5. 8-10 ; John 15. 16 ; I John 4. 10 and 19) applies in heightened measure to Baptism as reception into the Body of Christ. The grace of Baptism is not only a ' picture ' of *gratia praeveniens* which God has applied to us at

---

[1] This is emphasised also by G. Bornkamm: *Taufe und neues Leben bei Paulus* (Theol. Blätter, 1939, Sp. 237, n. 14).

Golgotha. It is more : a once-for-all event *entirely dependent on Golgotha*, and also a *new and special* manifestation of the *same gratia praeveniens*. The divine act of salvation advances into the time of the Church.

At Golgotha, the prevenient grace of God in Christ is apportioned to *all* men, and entry into Christ's kingdom is opened to them. In Baptism, entry is opened up to that place which I have elsewhere designated as the ' inner circle ' of this Kingdom, that is, to the earthly Body of Christ, the Church.[1] Golgotha and Baptism are related to one another as are the wider all-inclusive Kingdom of Christ and the Church. The *gratia baptismalis* is the special manifestation of one and the same *gratia praeveniens* apparent at Golgotha. That there is this special manifestation is connected with the fact that in the New Testament there is on the one side a humanity redeemed by Christ, and on the other a Church, a universal *Regnum Christi* and a narrower Body of Christ.

Protestant theologians manifest a manifold and much too exaggerated anxiety to formulate in another way the question from which we have set out. They ask whether Christ does not complete in the present, today, and each time, a *new work* at the moment of each individual Baptism in his Church, a new work which consists not merely in the proclamation of the historical deed of Christ. Of course, he does not every time die anew ; but he who sits now at God's right hand permits the person being baptised at this particular place, within his Church, to participate in what was done ἐφάπαξ on Good Friday and Easter ; and this participation occurs, not by means of the transmission of understanding and faith but rather through his being set at this special place, his Body.[2]

[1] For this reason, emergency Baptisms are meaningless. ˙A dying child will not belong to this earthly Body of Christ.

[2] Barth in his treatise has scrutinised the question what special thing happens in Baptism ; and he is at pains, in distinction from most teachers on Baptism, to affirm what special thing Baptism means in view of the once-for-all historical deed of Christ. He conceives the primary event in Baptism to be merely the *cognitio* of salvation ; according to him the incorporation of a man in the Body of Christ

Sheer anxiety about ' catholic ' or perhaps only ' Anglican ' or ' Lutheran ' interpretations must not prevent us raising the question about the *special* operation and *efficacy* of Christ within the Church with reference to any event, even that of Baptism ; nor should it compel us *a priori* to a negative answer. This would not be in accordance with the norms discoverable in the New Testament. It would be to mistake the all-embracing *Regnum Christi* for the much narrower Church in its particular setting.[1] For the wider circle of the *Regnum Christi* there is that one historical baptismal event at Golgotha. For the Church there is a special event in every act of Baptism. For all, whether baptised or not baptised, Christ died there. But for the members of the Church this same participation in the death and resurrection of Christ is connected with ' being baptised into the Body of Christ ' crucified and risen.

The event of Golgotha stands from the point of view of time and salvation in the same relation to the event of Baptism as to the event of the Eucharist. This means on the one side that Baptism is no kind of repetition of that historical once-for-all event, but an ever new event, which, whenever a member is ' added,' reminds us that salvation history continues in the present time. On the other hand, it means, of course, that this present event is entirely determined by the once-for-all event at Golgotha, the ἐφάπαξ of the centre of time.[2]

In view of what the New Testament declares about the Church as the Body of Christ, we may dare to affirm that in the divine plan of salvation participation in Christ's death and resurrection

constitutes, but not without this *cognitio*, the *fundamental*, divine and absolutely free act of grace in Baptism. But does he not thus allow himself to be led by the anxiety mentioned above, to deny to the event of Baptism in the present the character of a *new work* of Christ, which for the members of the Church in a special sense ' effects ' participation in Christ's death and resurrection at this particular place, the Church ?

[1] For this see my treatise *Königsherrschaft Christi und Kirche* (Theologische Studien, Vol. 10), 1941.

[2] For this see my explanations in *Christus und die Zeit*, 1945, where the need arose of showing how every salvation era both has its own value and remains connected to the central event.

is connected *with this place* not in an exclusive but certainly in a special way. On the basis of the divine economy, the Church is the locus of *the Holy Spirit*, even if this Spirit also ' blow where it listeth.' This does not mean that the members of the Church are preferred in matters of salvation to those not baptised, for whom also Christ is dead and risen. The special baptismal grace of those received into the Church of Christ consists rather in their being ' commissioned for special duty.' It is Barth's virtue that he emphasises this side of Baptism, and we take over the phrase from him. But we must again put to him the question why this ' commission to special duty ' in Baptism should be bound up with its being declared to the person baptised and at the same time accepted by him. In fact, it is itself grace : it effects the ' putting on of Christ ' (Gal. 3. 27), just as the incorporation of a young man in the army involves, as it were automatically, his being clothed in a uniform.[1]

It is infinitely worse for those who are baptised than for those who are not, if they fall from the participation in Christ's death and resurrection bestowed upon them at their reception into the Church, that is, in faith, the response which ought uncondition-ally to follow does not occur. It is in this connection that the New Testament words are to be understood, which speak of a sin which is not forgiven, for which no repentance is possible, as well as the kindred passages which talk of final exclusion from the community. Yet it still remains that even they who in this way lose baptismal grace from lack of faith continue under the sign of Baptism. Barth himself emphasises very strongly this *character indelibilis* of Baptism.[2] ' The whole teeming, evil humanity of western lands stands under this sign.'[3] But if lack of faith can destroy only the later effects of Baptism, and not the real event of the act of Baptism itself, it must from this be con-ceded that New Testament Baptism demands *subsequent*, not contemporaneous, faith.

[1] J. Leipoldt, op. cit., p. 60, tries to explain the ' putting on of Christ ' from the Mysteries.

[2] Op cit., p. 63. [3] K. Barth, op. cit., p. 60.

The opponents of infant Baptism often try to represent the matter as though every conception of Baptism which does not postulate faith as precondition presupposes necessarily either a *magic* or a merely *symbolic* efficacy, and that the alternative of magic or symbol can be avoided only in the case of the Baptism of adults, since in their case only a real and not a magical baptismal event is possible.[1] If we regard incorporation of the person baptised into the Church as a divine act of grace independent of man, magical understanding is excluded, since to *remain* in this grace depends upon the subsequent human response. This is to be explained more closely in the next chapter. Further we shall later see that in the act of Baptism itself the active rôle of the congregation excludes the *opus operatum*.[2] But here we will show *first* that the *act of Baptism* as such involves a real, and not a merely symbolic, event, although its further efficacy is wholly bound up with the subsequent faith of the person baptised and stands or falls with it.

We must distinguish very carefully between the reality of reception into the Church *at the moment of the baptismal act*, which represents a real grace independent of any perseverance, and the reality of the *further working out* of this incorporation, which represents a grace just as real but one dependent on perseverance.

I cannot think of a more adequate illustration of the first reality, that of the gracious act of reception, than that adduced by Barth[3] : the impartation of citizen's rights through the government of a State. But precisely this example explodes Barth's own view of the meaning of the event of Baptism. For what is fundamental in conferring citizen's rights is reception into the State concerned, not the declaration or recognition of the meaning of reception. The act as such has causal efficacy. It is not a matter of 'making known' but of a distinctive new thing happening. Every advantage that the particular State, on the ground of its historical acquisitions, has to offer to a man, is in

---

[1] So also F. Leenhardt, op. cit., p. 69. [2] V. inf., p. 54.
[3] Op. cit., p. 30f.

the act not merely promised to the new burgess as something to be safeguarded, but at the very moment of his naturalisation is *actually conferred* on him, whether he wishes or not, whether he understands or not. This act gives a quite precise and decisive direction to the life of the new burgess, whether he persevere in it or not, and is thus a very real act. Of course in most cases desire to be received is announced before the ceremony ; but this announcement is not part of the act itself, which is carried out by the government of the State. Barth forgets that even children not yet come of age and infants are granted citizenship without action on their part. Their civil life through this one act is really determined in just the same way, in virtue of the advantages effectively conferred and the duties effectively under-taken at that decisive moment. It is also to be remembered that after a war victorious States decree the collective incorporation into citizenship of the inhabitants of complete districts on the basis of peace treaties, without their declaring understanding or desire in the matter. But even this act has *just the same efficacy* as an incorporation into citizenship completed on the basis of an agreed proposal : it is for these citizens the same eminently real event, by which on the day of its accomplishment they enter into enjoyment of all the advantages of the nationality concerned, just as on them are thereby laid all the duties connected with it. Whether the consequences are just or unjust does not come under discussion here. We are only concerned to prove causal efficacy.

This example seems to me specially happy, because it raises the question of the event at the *moment* of the conferring of the certificate of citizenship. It appears that in this act it is only the government of the State that operates, in transmitting to the new burgess at the time of his reception all the advantages of the nationality. The citizen on his side remains passive. Infants and adults equally, whether with or without previous achievement, are affected by this act, and for both categories the act has the same momentous efficacy. From this it appears that the commitment of the newly received citizen, declared before or during the act, cannot be regarded as an essential precondition of the act. For both State and newly received citizen, maintenance of it subsequent to incorporation is important. But even in the case where maintenance is wanting, the act of naturalisation itself constitutes a very real and not merely a symbolical event. If the new citizen, whether infant or adult, by his practical conduct later repudiates the citizenship which is not merely declared in the certificate of citizenship but is forthwith with all material and spiritual privileges conferred upon him,[1] then those advantages effectively transmitted to him will lose their force for him. Then, by reason of that very act of incorporation into citizenship which can be carried out in independence of his will, he will become traitor to his country. It will be thus retrospectively confirmed that this act at the moment of its coming into force really effected a participation (now lost) in all that the State in virtue of its past represents, even if the citizen concerned was at that time inwardly opposed to it or had no understanding of what was being done.

Even if the parallel cannot be forced, it is still uncommonly appropriate for illustrating that Baptism as reception into the Body of Christ is a divine act independent of man's action, one which, in and with his being set within the Body of Christ, confers on the baptised person the grace that he ' be clothed with Christ ' (Gal. 3. 27 ; Rom. 6. 3ff) just at this particular place within the Body of Christ.

In this Body the resurrection power of the *Holy Spirit* operates. It is indeed constituted by it. Just as according to Paul sickness and death must even now be conquered by the completely worthy celebration of the Eucharist by a congregation (I Cor. 11. 30), so Baptism means being received into *the* Body into which the

---

[1] If we revert to the example of the inhabitants of a whole district, who in virtue of a peace treaty receive the nationality of the victorious State, without any action on their part, we can recollect that inhabitants, and also their children, *forthwith* are accorded enjoyment of the better rationing conditions which obtain in a victorious State.

miracle of the resurrection power of the Holy Spirit breaks through. Here, as we have seen, is the radical novelty of Christian Baptism, that in virtue of Good Friday and Easter Christ ' baptises with the Spirit.'

In this connection also, we have again to distinguish between the *further* operation of baptismal efficacy which follows the baptismal act and the thing that happens *during* the act itself. As to the first, the person newly baptised is set at the place where according to the primitive Christian view he finds himself forthwith in the realm of the Spirit, on condition of course that faith is present. In the gatherings of the congregation he is placed under special protection against the trials belonging to this final period of time in which he lives (Heb. 10. 25, see also Did. 16. 2). In the Eucharist of the congregation of the faithful he experiences ever and again the presence of Christ in this Spirit. Thus the baptised person receives the gifts of Baptism anew each day within the Church of Christ. The effects of Baptism as reception into the Body of Christ thus determine the whole of life. Hence the all-important *moment* when a man is once for all set by God at the place where such things occur must itself *in the very act of so placing him* possess the virtue of imparting the gift of Baptism. It is of this that we here speak. The appropriation of this gift of Baptism in the later life of the baptised person within the fellowship is dependent upon his faith. But this gift is already conferred on him without any co-operation on his part during and in the baptismal action, inasmuch as God incorporates him in the Body of Christ.

When Paul says we are baptised through one Spirit into the Body of Christ, he does not mean that the imparting of the Holy Spirit is a *precondition* of reception into the Church, though of course it is because of his free operation that he has already taken possession of a man (Acts 10. 44). Paul's meaning is rather that *in the act* of incorporation the Holy Spirit is operative. By reason of his nature the Holy Spirit is not imparted as a static quantity but only as something operating and *in actu*. His operation upon the baptised person at the moment of Baptism consists in ' adding ' him to the number of the faithful.

An objection might here be made. Is a man who is unable as yet either to understand or to have faith capable of even the passive *acceptance* of this baptismal gift ? This is not a question of whether the infant *must* die with Christ,[1] but rather a question of the possibility of the passive reception of the grace of incorporation in the Body of Christ through the Holy Spirit. We could simply retort with the counter-question : How could the event of Golgotha benefit all men, *when they had no faith* that they could thus be redeemed, or rather *manifestly disbelieved and denied it*? But in respect of the Holy Ghost there is present an obvious and special difficulty which we will not evade. Can the Holy Ghost operate on an infant which is not yet capable of faith ? Christian Baptism without the contemporaneous operation of the Spirit is unthinkable. Hence this question must be raised here, and some anticipation is necessary. There is no Christian Baptism without imparting of the Spirit ; and the earlier affirmation[2] is to be seriously reckoned with, that everything that at all pertains to Baptism must have its appropriate place in Infant Baptism.

In the accounts of Baptism in the Acts it is customary to adduce speaking with tongues as the immediate expression of the reception of the Holy Spirit in Baptism. In the case of infants,

---

[1] This question of the *guiltlessness* of children is a prior one, raised and much discussed since Augustine, in view of infant Baptism. Out of this arose doubt of the necessity for infants of a dying with Christ. The question is not directly answered in the New Testament. In modern times it has been the subject of essays by H. Windisch : *Zum Problem der Kindertaufe im Christentum* (Z.N.W., 1929, p. 119), and A. Oepke : *Th. W.B. z N.T.*, vol. I, p. 541. J. Jeremias, op. cit., p. 17, objects to Windisch that on the one hand Judaism never applied the conception of guiltless childhood to heathen children ; and further he recalls with Oepke that in Judaism, along with the doctrine of guiltless childhood, there was also the doctrine of evil impulse inherent in men from their mother's womb. The question is not of fundamental importance for our problem, if baptismal participation in the death and resurrection of Christ is regarded as reception into his crucified and risen Body. The ' seal ' of this reception must be received by every member.

[2] V. sup., p. 29.

such an effect is excluded. But this is not really significant, in so far as such an external and evident manifestation of the Spirit in those baptised in the New Testament, even for the adults amongst them, can by no means be postulated as necessary.

Further, it is really no deviation from our subject here if we refer to the hand of blessing, which the incarnate Jesus laid upon the children (Matt. 19. 13). For the evangelists, as I try to show in the appended chapter,[1] transmitted this tale with the evident intention of having it regarded as a standard for the discussion of the Baptism of infants, which was perhaps already acute.[2] It is also of prime importance to recall, in connection with the question here raised—whether an infant can be the object of the operation of the Holy Spirit—that this laying on of hands is precisely the gesture connected with Baptism which accompanies the *imparting of the Spirit*. Christ's hand, according to the evangelists laid in blessing on the children, is there the instrument of the Spirit, just like the hand which he laid on the sick. Those infants in the Gospels (βρέφη, Luke 18. 15) enter through the action of Jesus into fellowship with him. Certainly this is not Baptism ; yet this event from the very earliest times is quite rightly adduced as a legitimation of infant Baptism, in which nothing else is at stake than the reception of children into fellowship with Jesus Christ : ' Forbid them not ! ' Μὴ κωλύετε.

Is it not the effect of little faith and incompatible with the New Testament view of the efficacy of the Holy Spirit if this invisible miracle of the ingrafting of the child by the Holy Spirit into the community of Christ is regarded as impossible ?

But in so far as this miracle in Baptism is bound to the external completion of the baptismal operation, the objection of magic, of which we have already spoken,[3] could emerge. Here reference ought to be and *must* be made to the *faith* of the congregation assembled for the Baptism, which stands behind the operation of the Spirit. In the New Testament accounts of Baptism the visible congregation, which in time of need can be reduced to

[1] V. inf., p. 76ff.   [2] V. sup., p. 26n.   [3] V. sup., p. 37.

'two or three,' is absent only as an exception, as in the case of the eunuch (Acts 8. 26ff).[1] The faith of this congregation at the moment of Baptism *does not appear vicariously* for the faith of the infant which is lacking. This formulation appears to me unhappy.[2] It is wrongly applied to infant Baptism in the classic apologies, so that their critics have, also wrongly, only a 'vicarious' faith in view when they think of the rôle played by the faith of the adult members of the Church who are present at the administration of Baptism. In fact the matter at issue here in the faith of the Church is not that there be such faith as may do duty for a faith not yet present in the infant. It is that there be such faith as connects with the event happening to the infant being baptised, and has this end in view irrespective of whether the baptised person be infant or adult. If faith were lacking in the congregation assembled for the Baptism, it would not be a congregation; and then the Holy Spirit would be absent. But where the believing congregation is, there the Holy Spirit, operating within it and knowing no limitations, has the power to draw an infant into his sphere, just as in the case of all baptised persons who, according to Paul, are ' by one Spirit . . . baptised into one body ' of Christ.

In this connection, that is, as a function of the life of the community, marriage must be mentioned. According to Eph. 5. 22ff[3] marriage is honoured by reason of its integration into the Body of Christ. Hence[4] according to I Cor. 7. 14 the child of such a

[1] Even the speaking with tongues which usually makes its appearance presupposes the presence of a congregation, even if Paul in I Cor. 14 questions the value of this operation of the Spirit for the community, unless it be interpreted.

[2] This applies also to what is said on this subject by H. Grossmann, op. cit., p. 33f. ' Representation ' can only be spoken of in connection with the rather problematic ' Baptism for the dead,' I Cor. 15. 29. But the meaning of this passage remains on other accounts so obscure that it cannot be adduced for the illumination of the question of infant Baptism. But on this see K. L. Schmidt (*Kirchenblatt für die reformierte Schweiz*, 1942, p. 70f).

[3] H. Grossmann, op. cit., p. 20, rightly refers to the fact that even this passage concerns Baptism.

[4] On this see my essay La délivrance anticipée du corps humain d'après le Nouveau Testament in *Hommage et reconnaissance*. Rec. de Trav. publ. à l'occasion du 60me anniversaire de K. Barth, 1946, p. 31ff.

marriage of baptised parents belongs already automatically to the Body of Christ purely by reason of its birth; and we have already mentioned that this corresponds with the practice observed in the baptism of proselytes. This passage proves neither child nor adult Baptism. Both are unnecessary for the children of *Christian parents*, since Paul represents here the opinion that in their case sanctification through birth alone suffices. Even if this is not entirely certain,[1] this is probably the correct exegesis of the passage.

Since this passage, like those referring to the Baptism of whole houses, yields no unambiguous conclusion about the *practice* of Baptism either on one side or the other, it ought to be adduced in the debate in connection with the *doctrine* of Baptism only. From this standpoint, this text may certainly be said to presuppose an *idea of collective holiness*, even when the Baptism of these children is here regarded as dispensable — collective holiness in the sense of a *reception into the Body of Christ which follows not upon a personal decision* but upon birth from Christian parents, who have received Baptism. Then again this reception represents a divine act of grace independent of men. Thus, whether Paul here denotes the Baptism of a child as unnecessary or not, it is certain that *from the idea of holiness represented here there is a direct line to infant Baptism, but none to a Baptism based on a later decision of those sons and daughters who are born in a Christian home.* Thus, then, the hypothesis of Jeremias mentioned above, that the step to child Baptism was already taken in New Testament times, attains a high degree of probability even from this theoretical consideration.[2] This then denotes in the case of these Christian children not a transition from adult to child Baptism but a transition from the practice of the baptism of renunciation, analogous to proselyte baptism, to child Baptism which, in

[1] This is H. Grossmann's view, op. cit., p. 18, who mentions the 'holiness' of children on the contrary as proof of their Baptism. This seems to me unacceptable.

[2] Jeremias, op. cit., p. 24ff.

contrast to Baptism based on decision and profession, is founded on the same view of holiness as the renunciation of I Cor. 7. 14.

It should be closely observed that Paul in I Cor. 7. 14 speaks exclusively of children whose parents at the time of their birth are already Christian. The verse is on the other hand not applicable to the case of children of proselytised Jews or heathen ; but those verses speaking of the Baptism of whole houses are so applicable. We have seen that nothing certain can be concluded by way of proof of the actual occurrence of such child Baptism, though the practice of proselyte baptism lies close at hand. But from these passages we can at all events draw this conclusion concerning the doctrine of Baptism, that here also the solidarity of the family in Baptism is the decisive consideration, and not the individual decision of the single member.[1]

A baptismal grace valid for a whole community as such, namely, the people of Israel which passes through the Red Sea, is presupposed also in I Cor. 10. 1ff, a passage which ought to be much more carefully observed in the discussion of child Baptism. It is here quite plain that the act of grace, which is regarded as the type of Baptism, concerns the covenant which God made with the whole people.

In this connection, reference must be made to the continuity between that covenant which God concluded with Abraham on behalf of his people and the covenant of the Church which, as the Body of Christ, that is, of the 'one' (Gal. 3. 16), brings that covenant to fulfilment. The covenantal sign of the covenant concluded with Abraham, the circumcision, is denoted as the seal, σφραγίς. In Rom. 4. 11 it appears as the seal of Abraham's ' righteousness of faith ' in view of the community of all believers whose father he is destined to be (Rom. 4. 11b and 12). Baptism

---

[1] Barth, op. cit., p. 50, underestimates the significance of family connection in the New Testament. Of course marriage and family in the course of the time between the resurrection and the Parousia of Jesus have no kind of inherent value. But by reason of their integration into the Church they do indeed possess a value which does not belong to them in themselves. I Cor. 7 does not represent a fundamentally different position from Eph. 5. 22ff.

is even in New Testament times, and not only later, designated as σφραγίς. Hence the verb σφραγίζεσθαι (II Cor. 1. 22; Eph. 1. 13 and 4. 30). Like circumcision, the σφραγίς of Baptism is more than a ' copy ' or ' sign ' ; it is the seal which God impresses on the covenant with a community freely chosen by him.

We shall elucidate this connection in the chapter on circumcision and Baptism. Suffice it here to say that at this point we find the view confirmed, that the essence of the act of Baptism is the reception of a member into the divine covenant of grace of the Body of Christ, in whom the covenant with Abraham is fulfilled.

CHAPTER THREE

BAPTISM AND FAITH

IN the last chapter it was affirmed that Baptism involves two things : on the one hand what happens at the moment when the baptismal action takes place ; and on the other what results from Baptism, is determined by it, and extends through the whole life of the person baptised. The complete baptismal event is composed of not less than both these together. Accordingly we have now to distinguish between two questions : What part does faith play before and during Baptism ? and : What part does it play after ?

Is such a distinction justified on New Testament grounds ? The important passage relevant to this problem, I Cor. 10. 1ff, carefully distinguishes what happened in the course of the rescue of the people of Israel at the passage of the Red Sea, which is the prototype of Baptism, from the *further* occurrence implied by and dependent on this event, namely, the negative reaction on the part of the majority of the people to this Baptism and its tremendous consequences.

When the New Testament speaks about falling away from the grace of Baptism, as in Heb. 6. 6 and 10. 26, this distinction is evident. If one can irretrievably lose the grace of Baptism it is clear that the *later life* of the person baptised is critical for the act of Baptism. But on the other hand, as we have seen, the reality of what happens at the *moment of Baptism* cannot be contested.[1]

The authority for this distinction must next be indicated, and for this it is necessary to cite as further reference chapter 6 of the Epistle to the Romans, which stands rightly in the forefront of the modern debate on the subject. For when the indicative and the imperative of Baptism are connected in the way characteristic of this passage the whole matter turns on this distinction.

[1] V. sup., p. 37ff.

The Baptism of every individual is a *matter of saving action* from which further facts follow. We are, of course, at our birth already chosen in Christ. But within the mortal life of the person baptised, that is, of one who has been received into the Church of Jesus Christ, Baptism is the starting point of something that happens. Just as the whole of salvation history unfolds *in time*, so in the life of the individual there is an initial saving act, independent of natural birth, from which unfolding in time follows.

Hence Baptism in the New Testament is also called ' regeneration ' (Tit. 3. 5 ; see also John 3. 3ff) ; for it is a beginning, which is indeed in itself a reality, but to which a continuation belongs. It is thus like natural birth. For natural birth is a beginning which without any further extension represents a reality in itself, but which, deprived of its continuation, as in the case of an immediately supervening death, loses all further effectiveness despite this reality.

This New Testament distinction is most important for the question of infant Baptism, whose biblical character is usually contested on the ground that at the moment of the baptismal action faith is lacking in the baptised person. Is it not also a consequence of his conception of time that Karl Barth entirely omits to ask whether we must not deal with this temporal distinction in the case of baptismal faith ?[1] Must this faith really be contemporaneous with the act of Baptism ?

The designation of Baptism as ' regeneration ' justifies us in putting this question and in answering it in the negative. We have already seen that this second birth loses its *effectiveness* if death—in this case lack of faith—supervenes on the ' birth.' If it nevertheless *retains its reality* as a ' crucifixion of Jesus ' (Heb. 6. 6), that is, as a participation in the death of Christ realised *at the time*, the implication is that this unrepeatable baptismal act itself, this ' birth,' is not dependent on faith, and *neither stands nor falls* with faith. Only the subsequent life is so dependent.

[1] On this see Théo Preiss, op. cit., p. 116.

Baptism as birth must be taken seriously in the sense of a radical new beginning. The old no longer counts for anything—not even the faith already present; for the old man is at this point buried.

The important doctrine of Baptism in Rom. 6. 1ff does not refer to those not yet baptised. It presupposes Baptism as a salvation fact. It is not a baptismal catechism, but rather indicates subsequently to those already baptised (and indeed those baptised as adults) what happened to them in Baptism : ' reckon ye also yourselves to be dead indeed unto sin, but alive unto God through Jesus Christ our Lord ' (Rom. 6. 11). Accordingly this awareness of what happens in Baptism, together with the understanding and faith presupposed by it, is not part of the first act of the baptismal event but only of the subsequent and second act, even in the case of adult Baptism. Two things are thereby declared to the person baptised : You have been made the object of salvation ; and : Prove it now true, you that know it—and for Paul this means primarily : believe on the fact of salvation. Even if the Apostle here means only to remind his readers of what had been already imparted to them before Baptism, it remains true that he refers to persons baptised, and speaks of their Baptism as an event in the past, in which they were the merely passive object.

That prototype of Baptism, the crossing of the Red Sea of I Cor. 10. 1ff, is mentioned by Paul only to show that in the first act God is active, and in the second man must respond. The whole point of the connection of this event with Baptism is that afterwards, really and temporally afterwards, the response must follow—and this even when faith was already present before Baptism. This sequence of events : act of God—response of man—is normative. What happened to *all* (πάντες) the members of the people, namely, the miracle of God, is opposed to what happened to τινες, whom that miracle did not suffice to save, since they did not respond to it with faith but incurred the guilt of the sin mentioned there.

Thus it is confirmed that Baptism, so far as it is essentially a sacrament of reception, points to the future, and demands from the future a human response. This holds good for *all persons baptised*, whether as adults or children, and whether they had faith previous to Baptism or not. *My baptismal faith is not simply faith in Christ's work in general but on the quite specific deed which he performed upon me at the moment of my Baptism in my being received into the inner circle of his Kingdom, that is, into his earthly Body.*

But if it belongs unconditionally to the event of Baptism, that the person baptised, even when he believed before and during Baptism, should believe *afterwards*, what significance has it that in the majority of the cases cited in the New Testament faith also precedes Baptism as a presupposition ? The significance is to be found in this, that the New Testament, on grounds already mentioned, contains direct accounts only of the Baptism of adult heathen or Jews. In such cases, it is required that their reception into the Christian Church should take place only if at least the appropriate intention is already present on the basis of faith, to make the response demanded in the time that follows Baptism. The faith of the candidate is thus not a condition of the possibility of the divine action ; nor is it a guarantee of the future persever-ance of the person baptised. It is a sign for the Church and a criterion to baptised adults of their being chosen. In the case of the adult heathen or Jew, it is not his being born into a Christian family that indicates God's will to increase the Body of Christ by the ' addition ' of this man ; it is his personal faith in the Church. *This is the function of the faith demanded in the case of the Baptism of the adult.* It runs contrary to the meaning it has pleased God to give to Baptism if the Church undertakes the Baptism of a man indiscriminately, that is, *without any divine sign suggesting the prospect of his perseverance in Baptism within the community.* Such a Baptism would be just as contrary to reason as the so-called emergency Baptism of a child mortally sick. If he is not expected to belong to the earthly Body of Christ, then this necessary second act of the Baptismal event cannot follow.

An objection could here be made, that the case of the infant whose later reaction to Baptism is wholly uncertain is like that of the adult from whom a negative reaction, or just no reaction at all, is to be expected. In both cases Baptism would still have a meaning, in view of the possibilities that will later be open to them, of some time coming to faith. Thus the prior affirmation of faith, so often attested in the New Testament, would be also superfluous in the case of the adult if it had only the meaning which we have just accorded to it. Against this it should be observed that the case of the infant, as exhibited in the relevant New Testament texts, is so far different from that of an unbelieving adult, that the natural membership of a Christian family conferred on him by his birth, or at least the possession of Christian parents, by reason of the sanctifying and baptismal solidarity affirmed, is a sign for the Church that the divine baptismal event will in his case be completed, and that he will really be incorporated in the Church of Christ. In the case of an adult candidate coming over from heathenism or Judaism, the natural sign of birth is lacking. But his affirmation of faith has an analagous function to perform for the Church, and is for this reason indispensable : it shows the Church that God will operate within the Church of Christ, and by the Spirit baptises a man into it. The Church requires such a sign in order to avoid arbitrariness in the selection of persons to be baptised. This sign is provided for the Church by the birth of the child into a Christian family in the one case, and in the other by the faith of the adult.

Thus the confession of faith before Baptism on the part of the adult, and only in his case, is an element which belongs for these reasons to the ' ordering ' of Baptism, to adopt from Karl Barth an expression which he uses in another way. It receives its meaning from the necessity of faith *following* Baptism. Just as the possesion by a child of Christian parentage is indeed no guarantee of later faith, though indeed it is a *divine indication* of it, so too the faith confessed at the moment of Baptism by the adult heathen or Jew is no guarantee, though it is a divine indication of that *later faith* which is decisive. The affirmation of faith that precedes Baptism is thus not a constitutive element of the baptismal event incorporating a man into the Church of Christ. It is necessarily present only when, as in the earliest times was naturally far more frequent, the situation is one where the person to be baptised is an adult coming over from heathenism or Judaism. Faith *after* Baptism is demanded of *all* persons baptised ; from those adults just named it is demanded *also* before.

It is clear from the situation of primitive Christianity that in our earliest baptismal liturgy,[1] which develops into the later, affirmation of the faith in the form of a confession had an assured place, because it was designed for adults. From this we are unable to draw any conclusion about the meaning of Baptism. Jeremias has moreover rightly reminded us that even the liturgical and theological expressions in connection with proselyte baptism refer only to adults, though it is capable of proof that the children were baptised alongside of the proselytes who came over.[2]

Adult Baptism can therefore be held to be distinct from infant Baptism only in so far as prior confession of faith is demanded in the case of adults coming over from Judaism or heathenism. The doctrine of what happens in Baptism is nevertheless in both cases the same, since even with adults the faith that is to be confessed *after* Baptism by mouth and deed is decisive. Faith thus essentially belongs to the second and not to the first act of the event of Baptism.

This is confirmed by the fact that the New Testament knows of Baptisms—whether adult or infant makes no difference—which do *not* presuppose faith before and during the act itself. It is true that for reasons already given, which arise out of the concrete situations, the sequence in the majority of the New Testament texts is : verbal declaration—faith—Baptism ; but this order is by no means so strict as the opponents of infant Baptism affirm.[3]

---

[1] See Appendix, p. 71ff.
[2] J. Jeremias, op. cit., p. 17.
[3] See H. Grossmann, op. cit., p. 16.

In any case, where solidarity in Baptism on the basis of the New Testament connection between the family and the Body of Christ is presupposed, there can be no question of preceding instruction or of a faith present at the moment of Baptism on the part of the member of the family. This is certain, quite independently of the insoluble question whether there were infants in these ' houses ' or not. The story of the conversion of the gaoler of Philippi is instructive in this connection. Acts 16. 31 imposes the demand to believe upon the gaoler alone, but the salvation is promised to him *and his house* : ' Believe on the Lord Jesus, and thou shalt be saved, and thy house.' He is thereupon at that hour of the night παραχρῆμα baptised with his family, and he ' rejoiced, believing in God with all his house.'

We have seen that the idea of family solidarity in holiness, on the basis of the marriage tie and membership of the Body of Christ, is the fundamental ground of the declaration of I Cor. 7. 14, though Baptism is there regarded as dispensable. The Baptism of children born of Christian parents is based on the same idea of holiness.[1] Hence this passage must also be applied here in order to show that holiness, that is, *the fact of belonging to the ' saints,'* is bound up with those who, in the language of the New Testament, are *members of the Church of Christ*[2] and not with an already present faith.

Finally in this connection the Pauline prototype of Baptism, I Cor. 10. 1ff, must again be remembered. Here indeed it is not the relation between the family and the Body of Christ that is presupposed but the divine covenant contracted with a whole people. Was it perhaps Paul's meaning that this whole people, rescued at the Red Sea and ' baptised in Moses,' the whole lot of them, πάντες as he repeats with emphasis (vv. 1-4), had already without exception prior faith ?

The New Testament relation between faith and Baptism does

---

[1] V. sup., p. 44f.

[2] It is to be observed that I Cor. 7. 14 affirms that the unbelieving marriage partner alone is sanctified (ἡγίασται), while the children on the other hand are said to be holy (ἅγια).

not so unambiguously and indisputably affirm that faith leads to Baptism.   This is, of course, true of the cases recounted in the New Testament of adult heathen and Jews.   But for those other Baptisms mentioned, this sequence of events does not hold good. On the contrary, in them Baptism leads to faith, and this contrary order applies to *all* : Baptism is the starting point of faith. What applies to all must be regarded as fundamental.   In the class of individual adults who come over from Judaism or heathenism, we deal with a reverse operation :[1] faith brings them to Baptism, and Baptism, by which they are received into the community of Christ, leads them to faith.   The Church into which the baptised person is incorporated in the baptismal act is not only the place where the Holy Spirit completes the miracle but where he *awakes faith*.   With this we come to a last relation between faith and Baptism.

We saw in the previous chapter that the *faith of the congregation*, though not to be represented as vicarious faith, does yet at the moment of the baptismal event belong to the act of Baptism. Attention must here be drawn to the Church that *prays* for the person being baptised (Acts 8. 15).   It prays that God may complete the miracle of Baptism in the baptised person, whether adult or infant.   *This* faith which has the person baptised as its object is in fact an indispensable element in the baptismal act.

This is found to be confirmed by the rôle played by faith in the New Testament in the miracles effected by Jesus.   It is readily shown that at least in the Gospel according to St. John the sacraments have in the Church of Christ the same meaning as his miracles in the days of his flesh.[2]   For the Pauline parallel of I Cor. 10. 10ff the relation of miracle and sacrament is also fundamental.   From this standpoint it is justifiable to adduce, not as proof but as confirmation of the explanation here presented,

---

[1] S. G. Miegge, op. cit., p. 30ff.

[2] See *Urchristentum und Gottesdienst*, 1st edn., p. 33ff. ; Théo Preiss, op. cit., p. 119, rightly draws attention in this connection to John 7. 23, where Jesus accords circumcision a lifegiving power and draws a parallel between it and his miracles.

the fact that in the healing miracles performed by Jesus, on adults or on children, the decisive thing is certainly not always the faith of the person healed but the faith of those who bring the invalid to Jesus or inform our Lord about him : ' when Jesus saw *their* faith, he said unto the sick of the palsy, Son thy sins be forgiven thee ' (Mark 2. 5). It is indeed a leading theme of many healing miracles in the Gospels that the faith of those who beg Jesus for the healing of someone belonging to their house precedes the miracle. ' I have not found so great faith, no, not in Israel,' says Jesus to the captain of Capernaum (Matt. 8. 10), before he heals his servant ; and the stories of Mark 9. 14ff (Matt. 17. 14ff ; Luke 9. 37ff) are told by the evangelists in order to show that Christ is able to heal where there is faith. Here it is the father of the healed invalid who believes : ' If thou canst believe, all things are possible to him that believeth. And straightway *the father of the child* cried out, and said with tears, Lord, I believe ' (Mark 9. 23f) ; and on the other side, the unbelief of the *disciples* is blamed for their inability to heal the invalid : ' Why could not we cast him out ? . . . Because of your unbelief : for verily I say unto you, if ye have faith as a grain of mustard seed. . . .' (Matt. 17. 19f).

In the moment of the baptismal event the faith of the congregation present is likewise essential.

We therefore come to the following conclusion about the relation between faith and Baptism :

(1) *after* Baptism, faith is demanded of *all* those baptised ;

(2) *before* Baptism, the declaration of faith is a sign of the divine will that Baptism take place, demanded from *adults* who individually come over from Judaism or heathenism, but in other cases lacking ;

(3) *during* the baptismal act, faith is demanded of the praying *congregation.*

CHAPTER FOUR

BAPTISM AND CIRCUMCISION

IT was by intention and for reasons of method that in the foregoing chapters we first of all presented the New Testament doctrine of Baptism apart from the New Testament texts referring to circumcision. But this is not to accord these texts a merely secondary meaning. On the contrary, we shall now show that the doctrine and practice of circumcision, and of proselyte baptism which is closely bound up with it, are presuppositions for the whole complicated question of New Testament baptismal doctrine and its consequent practice.

These Jewish acts were performed both on adults and on infants—here the double practice is *certainly proved*. There is both infant and adult circumcision, and both adult and infant proselyte baptism. It is significant that in this regard Judaism experiences no difficulty. Here also, however, that other distinction has to be considered, which *mutatis mutandis* must as analogy be given weight when Christian baptismal doctrine is applied to children : the distinction between children born of Jewish parents and those who are taken over into the Jewish community with their proselyte parents.

First, it must be emphasised that the understanding of Christian Baptism as a fulfilment, and thus a repeal, of Jewish circumcision is not just a theological foundling, appearing only at a late date after the Apologist Justin ; nor is it just a supplement designed to support Christian Baptism. This conception is already present explicitly in Col. 2. 11, and implicitly especially in Rom. 2. 25ff, 4. 1ff; Gal. 3. 6ff and Eph. 2. 11ff).[1] A fundamental

---

[1] A significant essay on the last-mentioned citation has appeared : Harald Sahlin's *Omskärelsen i Kristus* (Svensk Teologisk Kvartalskrift, 1947, p. 11ff.). In agreement with an essay on Baptism in the Ep. to the Ephesians appearing in the same periodical (1945, p. 85ff.), he shows convincingly that Eph. 2. 11-22 is dominated by the parallelism between circumcision and Baptism, and he thus succeeds in explaining these verses, so hard to understand in a Pauline sense, in a satisfactory and congruous way.

kinship between circumcision and Christian Baptism is thus apparent.

The way in which Barth deals with this question is probably the weakest point in his doctrine of Baptism. Even if it is conceded that the Reformers' proofs of infant Baptism are not quite watertight, the Reformed argument at least merits more attention. Our modern knowledge, especially of New Testament writing, makes it the more necessary for us to let Christian Baptism be illuminated both formally and factually by circumcision and proselyte baptism. It is inexplicable to me how Barth, while conceding that Baptism is the fulfilment of circumcision, yet denies at the crucial point the inner relationship between the two, and can affirm that circumcision is in itself something quite different; so that the fact that children were circumcised has no bearing on the question of Christian infant Baptism. We shall in fact affirm a real correspondence; for Jewish circumcision is reception into the Old Covenant, just as Christian Baptism is reception into the New.

This correspondence is thrust upon us even by purely *terminological* considerations; for the New Testament applies the word σφραγίζεσθαι to Baptism, and on the other side characterises circumcision as σφραγίς.[1] Further it should be mentioned that circumcision is spoken of as a *being born again*;[2] and that the circumcised are called the ' holy,' as are later also the baptised. This shows clearly that circumcision is reception into the divine covenant of grace, and thereby accords holiness to the circumcised.

Barth believes he can invalidate the apparent New Testament relationship between Christian Baptism and Jewish circumcision, with the evidence it contains for the understanding of the nature of Baptism, by the observation that circumcision means being received into a merely natural racial succession and is applicable *therefore* only to male children. Hence no conclusion about Christian Baptism could be drawn; for in Baptism the determinative consideration is not connection with a natural

---

[1] V. sup., p. 45f. [2] V. (Strack-) Billerbeck, op. cit., II, 1924, p. 423.

succession, with family or people, but the faith of the individual. We can no longer maintain the view that vague reference is here made to Christian Baptism, or that in fact the New Testament recognises, as the sign of the divine will to salvation, in one case faith and decision and in another solidarity with a family.

But here Barth's view of Jewish circumcision must be contested. It does not at all agree with Paul's understanding of the Jewish act. According to Rom. 4. 11, Abraham ' received the sign of circumcision, a seal of the righteousness of the faith which he had yet being uncircumcised.' The faith of Abraham, for whose sign and seal God appointed circumcision, is directly connected with the divine promise given to Abraham, that he would be father of πολλὰ ἔθνη (Rom. 4. 17 and 18) ' of many nations,' not only, that is, of the Jewish people in its succeeding generations, even if the universal divine covenant, of which the father is Abraham, is begun with Isaac and his successors according to the flesh, and has Israel κατὰ σάρκα as its centre until the appearance of Christ. In Galatians (4. 21ff), the Apostle is at pains to show that the natural principle of succession according to the flesh is not determinative for the Abrahamic strain that is interpolated with Isaac. On the contrary : the son of the maidservant, Ishmael, is born κατὰ σάρκα in terms of the principle, while the son of the freewoman is born only through a miracle on the basis of promise. Thus Paul can characterise the Christians as κατὰ 'Ισαὰκ ἐπαγγελίας (Gal. 4. 28). If, in the view of the New Testament, circumcision is the seal of *this* faith of Abraham, thus from the outset envisaging the inclusion of the heathen world, then it is incompatible with the New Testament view of circumcision to see in this act only the reception into the natural succession. In fact circumcision is reception into the covenant, which God made on the basis of the promise to Abraham and his successors, to whom even the heathen belong, just as Christian Baptism is reception into the Body of Christ. The circumcision that is *rightly understood*, which takes place not merely outwardly

by the hand of man (Eph. 2. 11; Col. 2. 11) but which is
' circumcision of the heart ' (Rom. 2. 29), leads directly over into
Christian Baptism, that is, the ' circumcision of Christ ' (Col. 2. 11).
This is the sense of the explanations of Rom. 4. 1ff and Gal. 3. 6ff.
Even in the last-named passage the whole argument turns on
the question of the succession with which the promise to Abraham
is bound up; and here Paul expressly says that ' all born of
Christ ' belong to this succession. Thus Abraham, not in the
sense of natural succession but of divine salvation-history, is the
ancestor of the members of the Church of Christ. What holds
for Abraham holds also for circumcision, which he received on
the basis of the righteousness of his faith in the promise of this
succession. It too has its meaning for salvation-history, in as
much as it relates not to the natural succession but *a priori* to
the nations.

The starting point and centre of the divine covenant of grace
is, of course, Israel κατὰ σάρκα, on the basis of the divine choice.
But this is not decisive for the New Testament meaning of circumcision; nor is the quite correct recognition that ' the holy
lineage of Israel . . . with the birth of the Messiah achieved its
goal.'[1] It is rather the emphatic stress laid on the fact that circumcision is the *a priori* seal upon a covenant which is available
for all nations. That this seal does not remain a criterion of the
real members of the Abrahamic covenant, and that the boundary
line runs otherwise, is dependent not on its apparent orientation
to the natural succession but on the faithlessness of Israel. The
Pharisees, according to the familiar word of Jesus in Matt. 23. 15,
have made of the newly converted heathen whom they have
circumcised ' twofold more the child of hell ' than themselves.
Hence the ' entry ' of the heathen world has not yet been effectively
achieved. This has, however, nothing to do with the nature of
circumcision. The faithlessness does not consist in Israel's
misunderstanding in principle of the universal character of
circumcision, based as it is on promises. This universality had

[1] K. Barth, op. cit., p. 43.

in fact been applied to the heathen and had afforded them access to this seal. The course of salvation-history does not so run that only with the birth of the Messiah, in which the holy succession according to the flesh reaches its goal, did the divine covenant become available to the heathen. Hence the opposition Barth finds between circumcision and Baptism is false.

The characteristic thing about the *New Testament* doctrine of circumcision is then not the highly important salvation fact that Israel is chosen κατὰ σάρκα. It is rather its application to the nations. Despite all disloyalty, the Jewish conception and practice of circumcision, demonstrable at the time when Christ appeared, corresponds to this understanding of its essence. The very fact that long before the birth of the Messiah the heathen are invited to unite themselves with the covenant of promise proves that circumcision is not *even in practice* bound to the fleshly principle, and that accordingly one can say, neither of doctrine nor of practice in New Testament times, that 'circumcision refers to natural birth.'[1] Otherwise what sense would there be in characterising circumcision as ' second birth '?[2]

The Jewish *mission to the heathen* is one of the most significant expressions of vitality in the times of the New Testament. Did we not know it from Jewish texts, the New Testament itself would tell us that the Pharisees ' compass sea and land to make one proselyte ' (Matt. 23. 15). Neither these proselytes themselves nor their children stand in a succession guaranteed by natural birth. As a rule the proselytes are adults. On them adult circumcision is practised. Barth makes not the least mention of proselytes ; yet where the New Testament speaks of circumcision the adult circumcision of former heathen is just as often presupposed as the circumcision in childhood of the sons of Jewish parents. Paul's polemic directs itself chiefly (though not exclusively) against the demand that adult heathen coming into the Church of Christ must be circumcised. This also confirms our view that Jewish circumcision is by its nature not bound up with

[1] Barth, op. cit., p. 43.   [2] V. sup., p. 57n.2.

natural birth. In fact, its meaning is reception into the divine covenant, which is available to all.

The situation in this connection is *mutatis mutandis* the same as with Baptism. Access to circumcision as reception into this covenant is offered, on the one hand, to those who ' come in ' from outside (προσήλυτοι); and on the other hand to children who on the basis of their birth from Jewish parents are already destined for this community. For both categories circumcision has the very same meaning. In the case of children there is a difference only in so far as they are chosen not on the basis of instruction and decision but on the basis of their birth, which is divinely predetermined for circumcision. But this is just the distinction which we have found ourselves compelled in the previous two chapters to apply to Christian Baptism.

Circumcision is different only in this way, that in the long-constituted community of Judaism the necessity of child circumcision is naturally more frequent than is the opportunity of Christian infant Baptism in the newly emerging community of Christ. We have already seen from I Cor. 7. 14 that the question of the ' holiness ' of children was always arising for the early Christians. We remember that here Paul proclaims the holiness of Christian children on the ground of their natural birth. He consequently does not deem their Baptism as necessary [1] and he implicitly but completely precludes a supplementary adult Baptism of those children already born into the covenant of the saints. Just so in Judaism the adult circumcision of the children of circumcised fathers was precluded, though adult circumcision did exist. The analogy does not falter, because according to I Cor. 7. 14 the holiness of the children there envisaged is already guaranteed without their being baptised, while for Jewish children holiness according to the law only becomes effective through circumcision. For the decisive consideration is the fact that in I Cor. 7. 14, just as with the circumcision of the children of Jewish parents, the *motive power* to ' holiness,' i.e. to incor-

---

[1] V. sup., pp. 44f. and 53.

poration into the divine covenant, proceeds from natural birth. This is the rôle which natural birth plays in *both* cases. In both, it connects not with the essence of reception but rather fulfils with children of parents already received the same function as is discharged by the personal decision of faith on the part of adults coming over from outside, viz. that of a sign that God here performs the miracle of incorporation.

The analogy becomes clearer still if we observe that in New Testament times, in the case of proselytes to circumcision, a bath of purification is employed, the so-called *proselyte baptism*. It may be held as certain that John the Baptist is involved in this practice; but at the same time he introduced the revolutionary and —in Jewish eyes—scandalous innovation, that he demanded this baptism not only from heathen but from all circumcised Jews on reception into the messianic fellowship. Here already baptism seems to be superseding circumcision. For reception into the fellowship of those who desire to reckon seriously with purity in view of the expectation of the Messiah, John is already making no difference : all are now in the position of proselytes and stand in need of Baptism.

With the Jews, the act of reception for the children of the circumcised consisted hitherto in the *one* operation of circumcision. For proselytes coming over from heathenism, both adults and their children, there was added to this proper reception also the second operation, the baptism of purification. A difference between reception on the basis of birth and reception on the basis of personal decision appears only in this connection. It is primarily dependent on the Jewish purification regulations. We already mentioned the fact, important for our enquiry, that along with adult proselytes must have been baptised also those children of theirs who were *born before their conversion*.[1] In view of this practice and the contact of Johannine baptism—and therewith of Christian Baptism—with proselyte purificatory baptism, H.

---

[1] V. (Strack-)Billerbeck, op. cit., vol. I, 1922, p. 110ff.

Grossmann [1] says, quite correctly, that we should have to postulate in the New Testament an express prohibition of infant Baptism if this in fact contradicted the doctrine and practice of primitive Christianity.

It is not at all a counter argument against the congruity of infant Baptism with the Christian doctrine of Baptism, if we hear that John the Baptist demands repentance before Baptism. Since for him *all* about to be baptised are in the position of *proselytes*, he must demand *prior* repentance, in accordance with conclusions we have already drawn,[2] just as the Jewish missionary to the heathen had to call for the prior decision of the adult proselytes being won over. But we have not the least ground for believing that John had therefore, in contrast to Jewish proselyte baptism, shut out children who were brought to him at Jordan by repentant parents for simultaneous reception into the messianic fellowship. That we hear nothing of this in the New Testament signifies nothing against the direct contact of John with Jewish proselyte baptism in which this was the practice.

The other case provided for in proselyte baptism, where children are born *after* the conversion and *after* the baptism of their parents, could of course hardly occur in Johannine baptism, which was administered for so short a time. But of course it did occur in the Baptism of primitive Christianity, and we have seen that Paul in I Cor. 7. 14 follows Jewish doctrine and practice in this connection, according to which proselyte children are regarded as already pure and are relieved of Baptism, though they had to be circumcised.

In order to understand the deeper connection between circumcision, proselyte baptism, Johannine baptism and Christian Baptism, we must observe that John took over only one part of what for Jews was a double act in the reception of proselytes. He took over the purifying bath, since he was primarily concerned with the circumcised and considered that their unfaithfulness

[1] Op cit., p. 14.   [2] V. sup., p. 50f.

consisted in their conception of purity. So he must demand the purifying of all, even of those who were not proselytes. But since his baptism implies at the same time the *reception* into the divine covenant of all who penitently prepare themselves for the fulfilment of the ancient promise, the function of divine reception, hitherto discharged by circumcision, is now also accorded to the purifying bath. In this sense also the Johannine baptism prepared the way for Christian Baptism.

In fact it is characteristic of Christian Baptism that in it purity, i.e. the forgiveness of sins through Christ, is realised *in and through* reception into the community of Christ by the Holy Spirit. The demands for purity and for reception are no longer separated from one another into two acts. In Christian Baptism one becomes ' holy ' in the New Testament sense, in that he partakes in one and the same action of the redemptive act of Christ and is received into the fellowship of the ' saints.' Just like Johannine baptism, but as its fulfiment, Christian Baptism takes over at the same time the function of proselyte baptism *and* of circumcision.

If this essential connection is recognised, the hypothesis of J. Jeremias[1] attains a very high degree of probability. He maintains that the practice of I Cor. 7. 14, according to which Baptism was not demanded by reason of a holiness already attained through birth from a Christian parentage, could not be the last word in primitive Christianity. Christians could not be content with a renunciation of Baptism on analogy with proselyte baptism just because Christian Baptism implies not only the fulfilment of Jewish purification baptism but also of circumcision. The New Testament σφραγίς of Baptism, as fulfilment of the Old Testament σφραγίς of circumcision, must be imparted also to children who are already ' holy.' So in Judaism the ' already pure ' sons of proselytes were not baptised, but had to be circumcised.

Christian Baptism, by way of the Johannine baptism, took over the outward operation of the proselyte bath of purification from

[1] Op. cit., p. 24ff.

the Jewish practice of reception. But along with this operation, which in Judaism is only a supplementary act of purification for former heathen, it linked the meaning of circumcision as reception into God's covenant of grace.

This connection discloses the point at which Christian Baptism really begins to be the fulfilment of circumcision : the fact that the former in distinction to the latter can be and is completed on women. It has been emphasised that circumcision is not to be considered as for this reason an analogy to Baptism. But this argument does not take into account the affinity of Jewish proselyte baptism with circumcision. The ancient principle that only men are 'citizens with full rights' is in proselyte baptism already not so much by-passed as ruptured. If heathen women like men are permitted proselyte baptism, proselyte baptism was at least for women more than a supplementary purification rite. It was an incorporation into the Jewish community. Since the Baptism of the primitive Church superseded and fulfilled not only proselyte baptism but also circumcision as the act of reception, every difference between man and woman here disappears. At an even deeper level, this is related to the fact that the Holy Spirit, through whom persons baptised into *Christ* are incorporated into his Body, no longer permits the male to be singled out for favour (Acts 2. 17ff). So Paul in Gal. 3. 28, in a specific reference to Baptism, writes that there is no longer male and female. Thus the fact that circumcision pertains to male children alone provides no justification at all for contesting the connection of circumcision and Baptism, or for denying the analogy between infant circumcision and Christian infant Baptism.

Thus we further establish that, according to the New Testament, faith holds the same place in circumcision as in Christian Baptism.[1] In this regard the Pauline explanations in Rom. 4. are instructive, for they have as their direct object the problem of circumcision and faith. According to this chapter circumcision

[1] See chap. 3.

has to do with faith from the beginning. Hence Paul emphasises here that Abraham received this sign, according as he himself believed. He has no idea of saying thereby that the successors of Abraham also must *first* believe before they are circumcised. The Apostle knows very well that circumcision was practised on infants, who only *afterwards* were capable of belief, but it does not occur to him to criticise at this point. At the institution of circumcision, Abraham, as father of the faithful, had of course to believe, before receiving the seal of the divine promise, so that his position as founder and his relationship to the faithful might be visible. Just as Abraham believed on God's promise, so now his successors have to believe on the Abrahamic seal which they have been accorded through no act of their own. Thus it is by no means demanded of them that faith must precede reception of the seal. In view of the unambiguous connection between faith and circumcision in Paul's thought, the reference to New Testament criticism of circumcision really emerges as an argument in favour of Christian infant Baptism.

Abraham's faith, according to Paul, is faith in the miracle of the resurrection, which makes life out of death. For the patriarch believed on the promise that, in spite of the age of Sarah and himself, a son would be born to him (Rom. 4. 17ff). According to Rom. 4, circumcision is a direct *seal of Abraham's faith in the resurrection ; by his successors, however, it is administered to infants, who are capable of faith only after receiving it.*

It is thus evident that faith here, just as in Baptism, is thought of as in the first place a response, even though it is prior in the case of *adult* proselytes just as with adult ' candidates ' for Christian Baptism, and for the same reason. The affirmation of the necessity of subsequent evidence of faith leads us to the New Testament *criticism* of circumcision, or rather of its misuse. A distinction must be made between its pre-Christian misuse within Judaism and the post-Christian retention of this seal of the old covenant. The Pauline objection to the pre-Christian Jewish administration of circumcision is, as was said, not at all the practice of infant circumcision but that after their reception of this gift of grace the circumcised *proved failures*. What he writes about this in Rom. 2. 25ff fits in so well with what he says about Baptism in Rom. 6. 1ff and I Cor. 10. 1ff that one must conclude that the thought of Christian Baptism stands behind this chapter, though the reference is only to the unfaithfulness of the Jews and the divine seal of grace given them. Paul explains here that circumcision may not be conceived in a magical way, just as one may not 'rely' on the law (Rom. 2. 17), but that one must prove oneself on the basis of this gift. Thus circumcision is valuable: ὠφελεῖ (Rom. 2. 25).[1] Just as in the case of Christian Baptism, so here the sacramental operation is distinguished from the sacramental attestation, and we are constantly reminded of the connection between the indicative and the imperative of Baptism in Rom. 6. 1ff, and of the damaging consequences which according to I Cor. 10. 1ff even Baptism cannot stave off where attestation fails. When Barth writes that according to Rom. 4 the succession of those who believed on the Abrahamic promise even in pre-messianic Israel is not identical with the succession of the circumcised,[2] it must be objected, in addition to all earlier explanation, that the analogical affirmation is permissible for Baptism also, since attestation by faith is decisive *after* the reception of the gift of grace. If the succession of the circumcised is not coincident with that of the believing, this is due not to *circumcision* but to the *circumcised*. Hence Abraham was instituted as father of the circumcised and the uncircumcised according to God's determined plan to save, so that the boundary line now runs otherwise, as Eph. 2. 11ff, according to H. Sahlin's probably correct interpretation, shows.[3] Within Judaism there was a justified critique of the idea that the efficacy of circumcision is guaranteed by the externally completed operation alone. So there emerges the idea of ' circumcision of the heart ' (Jer. 9. 25f). Paul refers to this

---

[1] A positive valuation of circumcision appears also in John 7. 23. V. sup., p. 54, n. 2.
[2] Op. cit., p. 31.   [3] V. sup., p. 56n.

criticism also in Rom. 2. 29, when he sets the περιτομὴ ἐν σαρκί over against the περιτομὴ τῆς καρδίας, in which God deals with men and men respond to God. In Col. 2. 11 also, this criticism is presupposed, where circumcision is indirectly characterised as ' made with hands.' F. Leenhardt[1] tries to devalue the apposition of circumcision and Baptism clearly suggested here by saying that according to Paul circumcision is here a merely external act carried out by the hand of man, while Baptism is a putting off of the flesh in a really spiritual sense. But against this it is to be contested that Paul, like perhaps I Pet. 3. 21, also knows of a false conception of Baptism, of which he could say that it amounts only to bodily purification in water by the hand of man. In both places the external operation is not the important thing, and there is no real distinction at this point.

In Col. 2. 11 the Apostle indeed reckons only with this false external conception of circumcision. For he has in view here those who still hold on to circumcision even after the institution of Christian Baptism. With this we come to the criticism which the Apostle urges against the *post-Christian* practice of circumcision. After the covenant with Abraham, which was oriented towards Christ, has found its fulfilment in Christ's redemptive act, and participation in it is tied up with the relation between Jesus' Baptism by John and the Baptism of the Church, circumcision as an act of reception became pointless. For it is fulfilled in the ' circumcision of Christ.' Reception into the covenant of grace is now the result of Baptism, in that it purifies the person baptised from all the guilt of sin by permitting him participation in the death and resurrection of Christ. Where, moreover, the circumcision of the old covenant is still practised, it is not only meaningless but a slander against Christian Baptism, against God's plan of salvation. Here it ceases to be regarded as within the scope of the New Testament plan of salvation. Here it no longer points towards Christ but is discarded from God's plan of salvation, and is then evidently no more a seal of the faith of

[1] Op. cit., p. 67f.

Abraham in his faithful successors but a merely external rite, a tribal sign. Hence Paul must say to the Jews: 'they ought not to circumcise their *children*' (Acts 21. 21). If circumcision is further performed where Baptism into the death of Christ as incorporation into the Church of Christ is available to all men, God no longer operates through it: it is then in fact only externally 'done by the hand of man' (Col. 2. 11 and Eph. 2. 11); and in another passage Paul can even place it on a level with the self-mutilations of those professing heathen cults (Gal. 5. 12). Thus are explained the uncommonly strict words with which the Apostle lashes the retention of circumcision, while on the other hand in Rom. 2. 25, where he places himself at a pre-messianic standpoint, he can say: ὠφελεῖ. After Christ on the Cross procured a general Baptism, into which everyone since Pentecost can be baptised, those who still practise and administer circumcision act as if Christ were dead in vain (Gal. 5. 2ff).

If, however, circumcision is repealed only because there is now Baptism into Christ's death and resurrection as reception into the new covenant of Christ's Body, and if consequently Baptism is no radically new gift of grace, the suggestion is confirmed that the meaning of ' seal ' at one decisive point cannot be radically different from that at another. *This continuity according to Rom. 4 has to do with faith.* The successors of Abraham, *the natural like the proselyte*, are all to exercise the same faith in God's resurrection power both before and after the appearing of the Messiah ; for they owe their existence as believers to this faith of Abraham in the divine miracle which even without σάρξ can raise up successors (Rom. 4. 19 and Gal. 4. 21f), if need be, ' out of stones ' (Matt. 3. 9; Luke 3. 8), a word which belongs to this context. Therefore the place of faith remains the same: all successors of Abraham are to *respond* in faith to the divine grace which is offered to them without their co-operation, and which has set them, whether in virtue of circumcision or of Baptism, at the place appointed in salvation-history for the divine covenant, just as Abraham *responded* with faith to the promise of God.

E

CONCLUSION

IN the New Testament it is certainly proved that Baptism is applied to adult Jews and heathen who come over to Christianity. Proof of infant Baptism is at best indirectly demonstrable from observable indications. On the other hand, infant Baptism is in every detail congruous with the *doctrine* of Baptism, in the following ways :

(1) in so far as Christ in his death and resurrection procures for all men and independent of them a *general Baptism* ;

(2) in so far as God in the entirely sovereign act of grace of Church Baptism permits the person baptised, through an *incorporation* into the fellowship of the Body of Christ at a specific place, to take part in that once-for-all saving event ;

(3) in so far as *faith* as *response* to this grace is decisive ;

(4) in so far as Baptism in its nature is the completion of *circumcision* and of the *proselyte baptism* connected with it.

From these final conclusions, both adult and infant Baptism are to be regarded as equally biblical. I began this work in the belief that I should reach this unqualified conclusion. But I end the examination by adding a restriction : the Baptism of adults, whose parents at their birth were already believing Christians,[1] is not demonstrable. Moreover, a postponement of Baptism of this kind is incongruous with the New Testament presupposition, according to which, *in this special case*, it is not previous personal decision of faith (as in the case of proselyte heathen and Jews) but natural birth within the Church that is to be regarded as the sign of the divine will to salvation and consequently as claim to reception into the fellowship of Christ.

[1] The word ' believing ' is to be emphasised here. Where the parents are indeed baptised, but later fall from faith, the case alters, and then the postponement of New Testament Baptism is not only justified but demanded.

TRACES OF AN ANCIENT BAPTISMAL FORMULA IN THE NEW TESTAMENT

THE oldest baptismal ritual appears in Acts 8. 36-37.[1] As in all accounts of Baptism in the New Testament, the case here, in accordance with the situation of these earliest days, is one of adult Baptism. We have seen that in this case faith precedes Baptism and why it must so precede. It is probably an error to regard verse 37 as a later addition, though it is only attested by the Western Text and from this reaches the Antiochean Text. Replying to the question of the eunuch (verse 36), Philip here says to him : 'If thou believest with all thine heart, thou mayest [be baptised].' The eunuch replies : 'I believe that Jesus Christ is the Son of God.' This short confession refers to earliest times. For it is just on the occasion of Baptism that the confession was soon developed further, and, in consequence of the need to mention the Spirit as the baptismal gift, was broadened out into a three-membered formula.[2] Thus if we had in verse 37 only an interpretation influenced by later baptismal practice, we should not have had here a *brief* confession which takes us back to the earliest times. It is congruous with this that, according to the earliest texts, only the name of Christ is invoked even in the very act of Baptism.

Verse 37 in chapter 8 of the Acts appears to me, moreover, to contain the earliest baptismal ritual when it gives the liturgical answer, ἔξεστιν, to the question in verse 36 which itself, as we shall see, is liturgical in character. Certain baptismal accounts in the New Testament permit us to follow up the traces of this liturgical question, as it was customarily placed at the beginning of the baptismal ceremony even in the first century.

[1] V. sup., p. 52f.
[2] See O. Cullmann, *The Earliest Christian Confessions of Faith*, Eng. edn., 1948, pp. 43ff.

We choose three of the relevant texts from Acts, and one from the Gospel according to St. Matthew. To this last is added a corresponding text from the apocryphal Gospel of the Ebonites.[1]

(i) Acts 8. 36 : καί φησιν ὁ εὐνοῦχος· ἰδοὺ ὕδωρ· τί <u>κωλύει</u> με βαπτισθῆναι ;

And the eunuch said : See, here is water. What *doth hinder* me to be baptised ?

(ii) Acts 10. 47 : τότε ἀπεκρίθη Πέτρος· μήτι τὸ ὕδωρ δύναται κωλῦσαί τις τοῦ μὴ βαπτισθῆναι τούτους, οἵτινες τὸ πνεῦμα τὸ ἅγιον ἔλαβον ὡς καὶ ἡμεῖς ;

Peter said : Can any man *forbid* water, that these should not be baptised which have received the Holy Ghost as well as we ?

(iii) Acts 11. 17 : εἰ οὖν τὴν ἴσην δωρεὰν ἔδωκεν αὐτοῖς ὁ θεὸς ὡς καὶ ἡμῖν πιστεύσασιν ἐπὶ τὸν κύριον Ἰησοῦν Χριστόν, ἐγὼ τίς ἤμην δυνατὸς <u>κωλῦσαι</u> τὸν θεόν ;

Forasmuch then as God gave them the like gift as he did unto us, who believed on the Lord Jesus Christ, what was I, that I could *withstand* God ?

(iv) Matt. 3. 13f : τότε παραγίνεται ὁ Ἰησοῦς ἀπὸ τῆς Γαλιλαίας ἐπὶ τὸν Ἰορδάνην πρὸς τὸν Ἰωάννην τοῦ βαπτισθῆναι ὑπ' αὐτοῦ. ὁ δὲ <u>διεκώλυεν</u> αὐτὸν λέγων· ἐγὼ χρείαν ἔχω ὑπὸ σού βαπτισθῆναι.

Then cometh Jesus from Galilee to Jordan unto John, to be baptised of him. But John *forbad* him, saying, I have need to be baptised of thee.

(iva) Gospel of the Ebionites (Epiphanias 30. 13) : Ἰωάννης προσπεσὼν αὐτῷ ἔλεγε· δέομαί σου, κύριε, σύ με βάπτισον· ὁ δὲ <u>ἐκώλυσεν</u> αὐτὸν λέγων κτλ.

John fell down before Jesus, and said : I pray thee, Lord, baptise thou me. But Jesus *prevented* him, and said &c.

[1] We shall see that still another Gospel text must be taken into account. V. inf., p. 76ff.

In these texts it is striking how regularly the verb κωλύειν, 'prevent,' appears when Baptism is referred to. This observation is not without significance, and suggests the following consideration : Would not the question, whether anything prevented the Baptism of this or that candidate, be put from time to time in the first century before the completion of Baptism, so that gradually it became a ritual question ? Further, do not the accounts of Baptism in which the word κωλύειν appears with a certain regularity manifest a certain liturgical character ?

The question : ' What prevents me being baptised ? ' which appears in the account in Acts 8. 36, where it is rather surprisingly put by the eunuch, would then be explained. In fact a much simpler and more direct question would be expected here : ' Can I be baptised ? '[1] Ancient scholars were surprised by the peculiar form of the question. Chrysostom saw in it an expression from circumcision. Calvin did not accept this explanation, but draws attention to the fact that ' this question carries more weight than if he [the eunuch] had merely said to Philip : I wish you to baptise me ' (' ceste interrogation a plus de véhémence que si l'eunuque eust simplement dit à Philippe : je veux que tu me baptizes '). He tries to explain the peculiar word κωλύειν by the ' things which could prevent the reception of Baptism, that he in no case exhibit illwill or hate of the Queen or of the despised of his whole nation ' (' choses qui pouvoyent destourner l'eunuque de recevoir le Baptesme, afin qu'il ne s'exposast point à la malveillance et haine de la Royne ne aux opprobres de toute sa nation ').[2] This much too artificial exposition can by no means satisfy us. It appears more probable to us that the question of the eunuch represents a ritual question, which in the time of the author of Acts must have been frequently used.

The way in which the verb κωλύειν is introduced in Acts 10.47 is even more surprising. For here the water is what is

---

[1] It is, however, impossible to translate the Greek text τί κωλύει as ' can I not be baptised ? ' as H. W. Beyer does in his Commentary on Acts in *Das Neue Testamant Deutsch*, vol. 2, 1932, p. 57.
[2] Calvin : *Commentaires sur les Actes*, ad loc.

'prevented.'[1] 'Can any man forbid water...?' Although in Christian art of ancient days a personification of the water appears later in representations of Baptism,[2] we must recognise that this is not to be expected in our text, and that it calls for another explanation. According to the situation described in the context, it was water Baptism that is required, since the candidates had already received Spirit Baptism. In this special case, an effect had thus early appeared which normally only *followed* water Baptism.[3] Water is here regarded as bringing those to Baptism who had already received the Spirit. Peter explains that the request made by the water itself cannot be declined. This unusual personification of water is perhaps best explained by an ancient use according to which the person to be baptised is presented by a third party to the celebrant, who, according to the circumstances, accepts or declines the request made on behalf of the candidate. He explains either that there is no hindrance—οὐδὲν κωλύει or ἔξεστιν—or on the contrary that a hindrance exists.[4]

In the third passage (Acts 11. 17) the situation is the same. Only it is not the water but God himself who, because of the fact that he has already bestowed the Spirit on the candidates, is regarded as bringing them to Baptism. Peter's explanation has even more force than in the preceding chapter : the Apostle cannot decline a request which God himself makes on behalf of the heathen. In this special case, though there are parallels elsewhere, it is to be observed that the word κωλύειν is used almost

---

[1] Certainly there is here a personification of the water.

[2] Cabrol-Leclerq : *Dictionnaire d'Archéologie chrétienne et de Liturgie*, article Baptême.

[3] We have here an interesting attempt to underline the necessity of water Baptism and its connection with Spirit Baptism—and this at a time when both stood in danger of becoming two independent operations, immersion and laying on of hands. On this see above, p. 11ff.

[4] E. Preuschen : *The Book of the Acts* (Handbuch z.N.T.), 1912, p. 69, proposes to regard τὸ ὕδωρ as an interpolation, and proceeds : '*The thought in this case is erroneous, for it is the Apostle, not the water that is hindered.*' Preuschen here has misunderstood the situation which is the same as in chapter 11. 17. The Apostle is not regarded as in the first instance the one who is hindered but as the one who by the imposition of his veto can prevent water Baptism.

as a *terminus technicus* without indirect expansion. The Text D holds it necessary, after the words : ' what was I, that I could withstand God ? ' to add an infinitive : ' to give the Holy Spirit to those who believed on him ' (τοῦ μὴ δοῦναι αὐτοῖς πνεῦμα ἅγιον πιστεύσασιν ἐπ' αὐτῷ). The author of this variant has evidently mistaken the meaning of the sentence when he expands it thus. For according to the context, and above all to Acts 10. 47, ' hinder ' (withstand) must be expanded rather differently, thus : ' from also granting them water.' The version of Text D is certainly not original, whatever Preuschen says about it.[1]

It is to be recognised that the use of the word κωλύειν without any addition is irregular. The operation which must not be prevented (i.e. water Baptism) is not identical with what has just been mentioned (Spirit Baptism).[2] Yet this rather surprisingly defective infinitive construction after κωλύειν is readily explained if we understand this word as a *terminus technicus*, taken from the baptismal formula : ' What is to hinder so and so from being baptised ? ', or from the analogous formula whose influence is present also in Matt. 3. 14 and in the passage from the Gospel of the Ebionites.

From our comparison of the five passages, we therefore believe it possible to draw the following conclusion. As early as the first century, whenever someone who had come to faith was brought for Baptism, enquiry was made whether any hindrance existed, that is, whether the candidate had really fulfilled the conditions demanded.

The persistent emphasis in the accounts of Christian Baptism on the repentance and faith of the adults who receive Baptism allows us to conclude that, when former heathen or Jews came over to Christianity, this was one of the essential and universal conditions demanded.

But this was doubtless not the only demand imposed generally

[1] Op cit., ad loc.
[2] In other passages, such as Luke 9. 49 ; 11. 52 ; also Mark 10. 14, to which reference will be made on p. 76f, the situation is different, since the prior infinitive can be understood in what immediately precedes.

at the reception of Baptism. There are also other different conditions according to circumstances. In *Jewish Christian* communities it appears to have been the constant practice to enquire whether the candidate were a Jew, and to demand circumcision as an obligatory condition. It is against this practice that Peter is roused in the account in Acts 10 and 11. Against the Jewish Christian practice Peter gives a negative reply to the question whether uncircumcision is a hindrance to Baptism.

In every case, and whatever the conditions imposed, when conviction was reached that the candidate had fulfilled them, the declaration *nihil obstat* was certainly made before Baptism took place—οὐδὲν κωλύει[1] or ἔξεστιν as we read in Acts 8. 37. These forms answer the question : τί κωλύει 'What hinders?' (Acts 8. 36).

Another observation emerges from the passages : in spite of the regularity with which this question was apparently put, it was never quite fixed by whom it should be put. If the above passages be examined, we ascertain that according to the first and the fourth (Acts 8. 36 and Matt. 3. 14) it is the person about to be baptised who puts the question. According to the second and the third, however (Acts 10. 47 and Acts 11. 17), the question was put by a third party, who had the function of a kind of godparent (in the second passage, the water ; in the third, God himself).

As for the person who had to give the affirmative or negative reply, the five passages seem to designate the celebrant of the rite, though the second and third passages appear in the special case of Jewish Christians to presuppose a prior interrogation of those present.

We can add to the five passages which formed our starting point another passage from the synoptic Gospels : Mark 10. 13-16 and parallels. Though this account, which also contains the word κωλύειν 'hinder,' does not speak of Baptism but rather of the

---

[1] In secular Greek the expression οὐδὲν κωλύει has in fact this meaning. Cf. Plato: Gorgias 458 D and elsewhere.

blessing of children by laying on of hands, yet we think it necessary to mention it here. Tertullian had in fact already brought the question of infant Baptism into relation with this pericope, where Jesus demands that children be not hindered from coming to him, for theirs is the Kingdom of God. The way in which Tertullian speaks of this at least shows that those who practised infant Baptism used this account to support their practice. Tertullian criticises this practice. But even he recognises the account of Mark 10. 13-16 as a norm, and the question can be solved only when this account is rightly expounded. ' It is indeed true,' he arguos, in his writing on Baptism,[1] ' that our Lord said : Let them come unto me. They ought to come—but when they are older. They ought to come —but when they have learnt, when they have been instructed why they come ! ' This exposition can be justified, if need be, in Mark 10. 13 and Matt. 19. 13f, by reason of the expression παιδία, which, though it designates *little* children, does not exclusively refer to new-born children. But it is excluded by the Lukan parallel (18. 15), which speaks of βρέφη, infants.[2] However this may be, Tertullian did not at any rate contest the connection existing between this story and Baptism. This facilitated the task of opposing the Baptism of too young children which he set himself. This shows that the connection was recognised universally from the earliest days of Christianity. Calvin later in his commentary on the Harmony of the Gospels went so far as to name this story a ' defence against the Anabaptists ' ; and he speaks of it as though it were a story of Baptism.[3]

It is certain that originally it does not deal with Baptism. Yet it seems to us that this connection (which is resuscitated in another

[1] Tertullian : De baptismo 18.

[2] For this see J. Jeremias : *Hat die älteste Christenheit die Taufe geübt ?* p. 27, and Z.N.W., 1940 (Mark 10. 13-16 and parallels and the practice of infant Baptism in the primitive church), p. 245.

[3] Calvin : Commentary ad loc. Other passages in the article by J. D. Benoit, 'Calvin et le baptême des enfants' in the *Revue d'Histoire et de Philosophie religieuses*, 1937, p. 263.

form even by such modern scholars as H. Windisch)[1] does in any case contain a certain element of truth. We will not indeed aver that the question of infant Baptism was foreseen by Jesus ; nor that the primitive Church *invented* the occurrence of Mark 10. 13-16 to justify infant Baptism. On the contrary, we believe that the question of this practice emerged when the Gospel tradition was already fixed, and we agree with G. Wohlenberg and J. Jeremias[2] that those who transmitted this story of the blessing of children wished to recall to the remembrance of Christians of their time an occurrence by which they might be led to a solution of the question of infant Baptism. If this is so, we wholly understand that this story—without being related to Baptism—was fixed in such a way that a baptismal formula of the first century gleams through it.

These remarks lead us to quote the decisive verses of the passage in question, though we give them in this work the part of supporting an hypothesis which in our view is sufficiently grounded without it.

Mark 10. 13-14 : καὶ προσέφερον αὐτῷ παιδία ἵνα αὐτῶν ἅψηται· οἱ δὲ μαθηταὶ ἐπετίμησαν αὐτούς· ἰδὼν δὲ ὁ Ἰησοῦς ἠγανάκτησεν καὶ εἶπεν αὐτοῖς· ἄφετε τὰ παιδία ἔρχερθαι πρός με, μὴ κωλύετε αὐτά· τῶν γὰρ τοιούτων ἐστὶν ἡ βασιλεία τοῦ θεοῦ·	And they brought young children to him, that he should touch them ; and his disciples rebuked those that brought them. But when Jesus saw it, he was much displeased, and said, Suffer the little children to come unto me, and forbid them not : for of such is the kingdom of God.

The situation is just the same as in the baptismal stories, especially Acts 10. 47 and 11. 17, with this sole difference, that blessing by the laying on of hands takes the place of Baptism.

[1] H. Windisch : *Zum Problem der Kindertaufe im Urchristentum* (Z.N.W., 1929, p. 119f).

[2] G. Wohlenberg : Das Evangelium des Markus, 1910 (*Commentar zum Neuen Testament*, edited by T. Zahn), p. 272. See especially the works of Jeremias mentioned above, p. 41, note 1, and p. 77, note 2.

In fact all these elements are present here : (1) those who are to be blessed ; (2) those who make request for their blessing ; (3) those who wish to reject the request ; (4) the person who executes the blessing and, finally deciding its admissibility, accepts the request ; and (5) the formula : μὴ κωλύετε αὐτά ' forbid them not.'

The conclusion to be drawn from this exegetical investigation is that the passages cited prove the existence of one of the earliest baptismal formulas. Perhaps two of them also contain the earliest traces of a kind of godparenthood.

These elements possibly have their origin in Jewish Christianity, whose chief concern in it was not to offer Baptism to uncircumcised heathen. Although the situation there was quite different, it is interesting in this connection to remember the discussion of the rabbis about the Baptism of proselytes and about admission to this rite which was conceded only after circumcision had been performed. According to the regulations of the school of Hillel, a period of seven days had to elapse between the two rites. The presence of three witnesses was demanded.[1]

The accounts in Acts are evidence of a stage of development at which repentance and faith are the only conditions of admissibility to baptism for adult heathen or Jews in the sense of our exposition in chapter 2.

Later a Christian catechumenate was to be set up. The Church will then make trial of the uprightness of the candidates and of the purity of their intentions, and reject those who mean to pursue a calling incompatible with the status of a baptised Christian.[2] But it is above all necessary to demand a stricter definition of faith in Christ. The short formulas no longer suffice. The Church will demand from candidates for Baptism the appropriation of instruction attested by witnesses. This will

[1] See the texts in Strack-Billerbeck, *Kommentar z. N.T. aus Talmud und Midrasch*, vol. 1 : the Gospel according to St. Matthew, München, 1922, p. 101-112.

[2] Tertullian : *De baptismo* 18 (Migne *scr. lat.*, vol. 1, col. 1221) and Augustine : *De fide et operibus*, I (Migne *scr. lat.*, vol. 40, col. 197).

be the external condition whose realisation will result in nothing 'hindering' Baptism any longer. The place of the simple ritual question is taken by an institution with a complete organisation whose smallest detail will be regulated.[1]

[1]See especially the Catechisms of Cyril (Migne *ser. græc.*, vol. 33, col. 348ff). Perhaps a trace of our formula is to be found in the Procatechism 3. 5. Cyril underlines there the meaning of the internal condition in which the new convert enters into his catechumenate. Paraphrasing the parable from Matt. 22. 11, he makes the king say : ' My friend, how have you entered here ? Did the doorkeeper not *hinder* you ?' Ὁ θυρωρὸς οὐκ ἐκώλυσεν;

INDEX OF BIBLICAL REFERENCES

Index of Biblical References

Index of Biblical References

INDEX OF NAMES